Kildare and Gillespie—three pairs of actors have played the Max Brand-created characters. They are Lionel Barrymore and Lew Ayres (top left) from the movies and the 1950-51 radio series *The Story of Dr. Kildare*; Raymond Massey and Richard Chamberlain (top right) from the 1961-65 TV series and Gary Merrill and Mark Jenkins from the early 1970s syndicated series that ran one season.

The
Dr.Kildare
Scrapbook

A Guide
to the
Radio and Television
Series

Gerald D. Wilson

BearManor Media

Duncan, Oklahoma

Published in the USA by:
BearManor Media
PO Box 1129
Duncan, OK 73534-1129
www.BearManorMedia.com

ISBN 1-59393-635-4
ISBN-13: 978-1-59393-635-8

Printed in the United States.

Design and Layout by Allan T. Duffin.

DEDICATION

To my wife Amy, who is a better wife than I deserve,
and to Ken Berry, whose Kildare memories and friendship
are very special.

Table of Contents

Acknowledgments

As Martin Grams Jr. told me when we working on *The Railroad Hour* book (plug), even when a book carries only one author's name, there are many people who helped. Martin's advice, as always, was very helpful.

Mother Nature cancelled our trip to the University of Iowa Archives during the summer of 2008, but Kathryn Hodson, its Special Collections director, was very helpful. The pictures in the volume, unless otherwise marked, come from Papers of Norman Felton, University of Iowa Libraries, Iowa City, Iowa.

Unless otherwise noted, information on episodes marked with a star (*) in the TV episode chapters were provided by the University of Iowa Library Archives. Other institutions will be cited for their contributions as necessary.

Felton, whose Arena Productions produced not just *Dr. Kildare,* but *The Eleventh Hour, The Lieutenant, The Man from U.N.C.L.E, The Girl from U.N.C.L.E.* and the *Psychiatrist* arc of *Four-In-One,* was an alumnus of the University of Iowa.

As noted in the dedication, Ken Berry shared his recollections of *Dr. Kildare* on which he was a semi-regular until he joined the cast of *F Troop.*

Bradford Dillman shared his memories of playing one of the few human foes Kildare met during the show's five seasons.

Heidi Hilliker of Metro-Goldwyn-Mayer's Intellectual Property department and that firm allowed use of its name in this volume.

I thank Steve Darnall of *Nostaglia Digest Magazine* for his encouragement while I worked on this project.

Gratitude to TV Guide.com for details on the few episodes I didn't watch and TV Guide for listing *Kildare* as #10 on its list of the Sexiest TV Doctors of All Time. Thanks also to Warner Bros. and to Sandy Grabman at BearManor Media.

And last but not least, my thanks to Ben Ohmart, who has been not just a publisher but a friend. I'm grateful to God for my writing gift ... but it's Ben who has allowed me to share it with the world.

Introduction

Although this book is devoted to examining the radio and TV adventures of Dr. James Kildare, he actually first saw life in the story "Internes Can't Take Money" (*Cosmopolitan Magazine*, March 1936) by Max Brand. A debt of gratitude is owed to Golden West Literary Agency, which controls Brand's printed material still, and releases new works for this generation to enjoy the work of the creator of Dr. Kildare.

Jimmy Kildare used to get away from the hospital every afternoon and go over to Tom McGuire's saloon on the avenue. He always drank two beers. An intern in the accident room has to have his brains in his fingertips in good order all day long, but two beers don't get very far between a man and himself if he has a bit of head on his shoulders ... and Jimmy Kildare had.

The story made its way to the screen in 1937 as the only Kildare movie not released by Metro-Goldwyn-Mayer. Joel McCrea was actually the first actor to play Kildare. His co-stars included Barbara Stanwyck and Lloyd Nolan. The film was released by Paramount Pictures.

The 1966 show used the saloon from Brand's first story, calling it Mac's. The radio show, which we examine in Chapter One, made reference to the movies but not Brand's story. According to Jon Tuska of Golden West, Brand (who died in 1943) sold the character to M-G-M but they still allowed him to publish the stories from the films in novel form.

But now it's time to call Dr. Kildare.

Lionel Barrymore and Lew Ayres.

Chapter 1

Kildare
on the Radio

A s part of its bringing some of its most famous movie series to radio, MGM put the team of Lew Ayres and Lionel Barrymore from the *Dr. Kildare* movies back together for a radio series called *The Story of Dr. Kildare.* It premiered on February 1, 1950, on WMGM in New York. Also included in the show cast were Virginia Gregg as Nurse Parker and Ted Osborne as Dr. Carew, the administrator at Blair General Hospital.

The major difference between the radio and TV series is that the radio series was set in New York City while the TV series was set in California.

1. "Angela Kester" February 1, 1950

"Blair General Hospital—where life begins and ends." These words were used by Ayres at the opening of each episode. This episode, like many others in the radio series, was named after the patient Kildare and Gillespie treated in that episode.

Angela believes that her husband Steven wants to kill her. When Steven takes Kildare out to the estate, he tells Kildare that Angela is a concert pianist who has been working too hard.

After Angela tries to commit suicide, Gillespie and Kildare must consider a risky brain operation to save her.

Writer: James Moser, who later created a TV medical series, *Ben Casey.* He also directed the medical series *Medic* which starred Richard Boone.

Director: William P. Rousseau, until episode 53.

Music: Walter Schumann.

Medical notes: Most episodes, except where indicated, were written by Les Crutchfield. The *Radio Goldindex* lists 290 radio credits for Crutchfield including episodes of *Escape, The Man Called X, Romance* and *Gunsmoke.*

2. "Marjorie Northup" February 8, 1950

Wyman, a hospital orderly, and Dr. Morton pick up a woman at the scene of an auto accident. However, they can't find any identification on her and Kildare says her right leg must be amputated.

Three months pass and the patient whom Kildare knows as Marjorie Northup hates him. Her fiance, Willard Mason, tries to see her but Marjorie orders him to leave. Gillespie takes over the case and a woman named Evelyn Williams, who also lost a leg in a car accident, helps Northup learn to walk again.

3. "Benjamin Barkley" February 15, 1950

A slightly ill Dr. Gillespie threatens to cut off Parker's nose if she doesn't keep it out of his business. Gillespie and Kildare both agree that the older doctor is suffering from the flu, and then discuss the wealthy Barkley, one of Gillespie's patients. Kildare thinks Barkley is suffering from appendicitis.

Kildare has a new nurse, who's had an appendectomy herself, to discuss the surgery with Barkley while he and Parker conspire to keep Gillespie in bed.

Trivia: Georgia Ellis ("Kitty" on radio's Gunsmoke) joined the cast as Nurse Diana Verner.

4. "Enrico and Carmen Machiano" February 22, 1950

Machiano asks Gillespie and Kildare for help in treating his sick wife. The doctors discover that Carmen is suffering from cancer and discuss how much time she has left as Gillespie says there is nothing they can do for her.

The doctors discuss their feelings for the couple after Carmen admits worrying about what will happen to Enrico and their son Tony after she dies. Kildare tries to help Tony reconcile with his father.

Carmen dies listening to Rico playing his violin outside the hospital. Later, Kildare and Gillespie discuss why they became doctors.

Featured: Jay Novello, Peggy Webber and Peter Leeds.

5. "Vernon Pendleton" March 1, 1950

Pendleton (Joseph Kearns), a wealthy hypochondriac and a member of the Blair board, is coming to see Gillespie. Gillespie transfers his case to Kildare, who discovers that Pendleton is in fine physical condition. Pendleton then goes over Kildare's head and complains to Carew.

When Pendleton is admitted to the hospital, Kildare and Parker concoct a plan to cure him of his hypochondria with some help from Gillespie. This results in Carew assigning Kildare to all such future cases.

Writer: Jean Holloway.

6. "Barbara Lane" March 8, 1950

Kildare's newest patient, Lane, becomes upset when he delves into her background. Gillespie and Kildare discuss her case when a man named Lane arrives but they discover two things—that Lane is not his real name and that Barbara is an addict.

This leads to the doctors discussing the morphine addiction of Sherlock Holmes. They discover with the aid of Clancy, the pharmacy manager, that the hospital's morphine supply has been stolen. The doctors and ambulance driver Weyman discover that Lane is really Barbara's drug supplier while Barbara threatens to commit suicide. Gillespie dissuades her by telling Barbara what a jumper looks like after death.

Featured: Barbara Ruick, Parley Baer.

7. "Carolyn Shelley" March 5, 1950

Despite Gillespie's diagnosing Carolyn as suffering from appendicitis, the little girl's governess doesn't think she is sick. Kildare tries to find the girl's mother (her parents are separated) and later goes to Carolyn's home where he finds the governess has given Carolyn castor oil against Gillespie's advice. He tells Gillespie that the girl needs an operation immediately.

Gillespie talks with Carolyn's parents while Kildare performs the operation. Later on, Kildare hears Gillespie ordering toys for Carolyn including a doll that wets his bed.

Writer: Jean Holloway.

Featured: Lurene Tuttle, Bea Benadaret, Marlene Ames and Jack Edwards.

8. "Janet Dane" March 15, 1950

Kildare is in charge of Blair's newest cancer treatment. Dane is his first patient and Kildare explains that she would only survive for six months without the treatment.

The doctors and Weyman watch the first treatment and Kildare calls Janet the perfect patient. Janet falls in love with Kildare but later marries a research doctor at a nearby hospital.

There are no details available on episodes nine and ten.

11. "Warren Jackson" April 19, 1950

The doctors try and discover why Jackson tried to commit suicide as he is newly married and a successful insurance agent. His wife tries to see him but Jackson, who is a very sick man according to tests run on him by Gillespie, doesn't want to see her.

Meanwhile, Gillespie is insistent on not letting Kildare examine him. When he gives in, Kildare puts his supervisor in an isolation room and takes over the Jackson case. Kildare believes an allergy is the reason for Jackson's condition.

Nurse Byrd tells Kildare that Gillespie, who has the mumps, is being a difficult patient. Gillespie sees the Jacksons before they leave and says he's developing an allergy to Kildare. Kildare winds up catching the mumps from Gillespie.

Writer: Jean Holloway.

12. "Terry Murphy" April 19, 1950

Despite Gillespie's disapproval, Kildare agrees to help a Blair cleaning woman whose grandson is facing a juvenile court hearing. However, when Carew tells Kildare not to interfere, Gillespie decides to aid Kildare.

The doctors talk with Judge Bryon about Terry and Kildare reveals how he's changed in the past year. Kildare and Terry discuss his crime while Kildare is giving him an intelligence test. Parker later reveals that she thinks Terry took a scalpel from her desk.

The doctors and Parker discuss the situation and Kildare thinks Terry has a problem with his hearing. An operation helps Terry get better.

Featured: Peggy Webber, Terry Barber.

13. "Philip Van Court" April 26, 1950

Carew assigns the doctors to find Van Court, a veteran suffering from mental problems. His parents leave a picture of the man with Kildare and Gillespie.

Kildare goes to Brighton Beach, where Philip's car was found, while Gillespie sees the police. Mike, an area resident, offers to help Kildare search for Philip, who is suffering from amnesia.

Irene Howard, a friend of Philip's, tells Gillespie that she is in love with him. Kildare explains the psychotherapy technique during which Philip remembers a wartime incident during which his best friend was killed.

Writer: Jean Holloway.
Featured: Sam Edwards.

14. "The Abandoned Baby" May 3, 1950

Weyman finds a baby in his ambulance. The doctors and Parker care for it and Gillespie says the baby is suffering from malnutrition.

Lt. Dan Riley (Jack Webb) and Kildare discuss the situation. Gillespie tells Kildare how he's treating the baby while Riley finds where the baby's mother was living. Kildare and Riley search cafes in the area. Riley later calls and says a woman has been pulled from the harbor.

Weyman applies CPR to the woman whose name is Eleanor Mason and Kildare talks to her about the baby. Gillespie says the baby will be all right.

Also featured: Edwin Max, Lillian Buyeff and Jerry Hausner.

15. "Jan Norman" May 10, 1950

Norman, a girl from Kildare's old hometown, has a date with him at the Central Park Zoo. The doctors examine her when she has a dizzy spell after they meet Gillespie and Byrd at the restaurant they go to.

Jan is admitted to the hospital and Kildare proposes to her. Gillespie discovers that a recent bout with the flu has caused Jan to develop a heart condition. When she dies, Kildare doesn't want to be a doctor anymore but her brother Bob decides to become a heart surgeon so he can help people like Jan.

Gillespie changes Kildare's mind and they go out to dinner with Bob.

Writer: Jean Holloway.

Featured: Lurene Tuttle, Eleanor Audley and Skip Homeier.

16. "Nurse Parker" May 17, 1950

Parker quits after Gillespie needles her one too many times. Kildare suggests that Gillespie apologize to her just before Dr. Carew comes in while a patient demands that Gillespie get Parker back on staff. (We learn during this episode that Parker's first name is Evangeline.)

Kildare maneuvers Carew into "helping" with the situation by saying Gillespie is acting like a spoiled child.

Gillespie confronts Carew while Kildare reminds Carew of his role in Parker's leaving. Parker does return and at first, she and Gillespie treat each other formally. However, Kildare and Byrd overhear them arguing shortly thereafter.

Featured: Peggy Webber, Eleanor Audley and Wilms Herbert.

17. "Angela Carew" May 24, 1950

Carew asks the doctors for help in getting his wife to lose weight. She wants to dance at a hospital benefit in two months. The doctors find that Angela weighs 150 pounds and design a diet with the help of Dr. Bromley.

Kildare discovers that Mrs. Carew has been cheating on her diet and reports this to Bromley and Gillespie. Bromley suggests that Dr. Carew promise his wife a mink coat if she loses weight. Carew agrees but requires the three doctors to diet and exercise with Angela and this gets her down to 118 pounds. The three doctors order large meals at a nearby restaurant after the dieting is over.

Writer: Jean Holloway.

Featured: Eleanor Audley, Herb Ellis, Jay Novello and Anne Stone.

18. "Dick Brennan" May 31, 1950

Kildare agrees to help Brennan, an old friend, prove his innocence when he is accused of stealing $50,000 from the Wall Street firm of Kessel and Conrad, Importers. Gillespie wonders why Kildare is helping Brennan and interrogates Brennan.

Captain Daggett (William Conrad), the detective investigating the case, and Kildare develop a plan to aid Brennan by playing on Kessel's hypochondria.

Also featured: Bill Tracy, Herb Butterfield.

19. "Colonel Beauregard" June 1, 1950

The show moved from Wednesday to Thursday as of this episode, which featured Conrad as the title character, who plans to sue Blair because of the treatment he's been receiving. He suffers a relapse when his daughter Emmy Lou, who is married to a reporter, tells him about the marriage.

The doctors believe that Beauregard's illness is psychoneurotic in nature and might be cured when he finds out about his daughter's pregnancy. However, he gets sick again when he discovers the last name of his new son-in-law is Grant.

Also featured: Jane Webb.

Trivia: Near the end of *Blitz Wolf* (Tex Avery's first MGM cartoon from 1942), the Adolf Wolf character cries out "Calling Dr. Kildare," a reference to the movie series.

20. "Gordon Mallory" June 8, 1950

Kildare and Gillespie suspect that Mallory, a construction site painter, is suffering from lead poisoning when he tells them about abdominal pains he has been suffering. When they talk with Sid Farrell, the site foreman, they find that Farrell was planning to lay off Mallory at the end of the week.

The doctors tell Mrs. Mallory that a dietary regimen and medication will aid her husband. After one of Mallory's co-workers is brought to the hospital with the same symptoms, Farrell allows them to tour the site. He later comes to the hospital suffering not from lead poisoning, not indigestion.

Writer: Jean Holloway.

Guests: Eleanor Audley, Dick Simmons, Tony Barrett, Jack Petruzzi and Lillian Buyeff.

21. "Greg Simmons" June 15, 1950

Simmons, who is facing blindness, may need an operation and Simmons says he doesn't want to live if the operation is not successful. After Simmons is sent home, his wife Dorothy calls and says he tried to commit suicide.

Kildare has Maria Espinosa, who lost her sight in the car accident that killed her husband, help Simmons adjust to life without sight.

Writer: Jean Holloway.

Guests: Isabel Jewell, Bill Johnstone and Peggy Webber.

22. "Priscilla's Broken Arm" June 22, 1950

Carew and Gillespie argue about Priscilla Babcock's broken arm. Meanwhile, Kildare discovers that Priscilla broke it while trying to escape from her school on Long Island and that she has been lying to them about her life.

Carew and Kildare make fun of Mrs. Babcock's interest in Gillespie. She is a former specialty dancer while the late Mr. Babcock was a bathtub manufacturer.

The doctors maneuver Carew into showing an interest in Mrs. Babcock and he convinces her to place Priscilla, who has fallen in love with Kildare, to place Priscilla in a new school where she becomes interested in a fellow student.

Guests: Sarah Selby and Pattee Chapman.

23. "Millicent Forbes" June 29, 1950

Forbes, a new member of the hospital board, invites Gillespie out to dinner. The doctors later examine her for a cold at Carew's insistence.

Kildare finds Gillespie's situation amusing but agrees to help him out of it. Millicent ends the relationship when Kildare tells her what the life of a doctor's wife is like. Kildare says Gillespie whom he calls the "Clark Gable of Blair General Hospital" should get married to Nurse Molly Byrd.

Writer: Jean Holloway.

Guests: Eleanor Audley, Isabel Randolph and Eddie Fields.

24. "Epidemic" July 6, 1950

The doctors go on a fishing trip in an area where Kildare spent a lot of time growing up. They encounter an epidemic that has already killed five children, according to area resident Ezra Riley.

Molly Byrd and Dr. Bob Wheeler, a surgeon who fell apart during a procedure, come to aid Kildare and Gillespie. Wheeler performs a surgery that saves a child's life just before Carew arrives to aid his colleagues. Kildare later suggests that Wheeler practice medicine in the town they're working in.

Writer: Jean Holloway.

Guest stars: David Ellis, Isabel Jewell and Ken Christy.

25. "Dan Malloy" July 13, 1950

The doctors discover that Malloy has a peptic ulcer and Kildare suspects the illness might be psychosomatic in nature. Gillespie, who has met Mrs. Malloy, thinks she might be the cause of her husband's condition.

Mrs. Malloy disagrees with Kildare's suggestion that the couple need to get away from the city, possibly to a property that Malloy bought on the Canadian border. Carew winds up buying the property. When a plan by Parker and the doctors result in Malloy keeping his property, the couple later send a package of lake trout to Carew.

Guests: Sarah Selby and Ed Begley.

26. "The Stanford Case" July 20, 1950

The doctors discuss Mrs. Stanford's heart condition with Everett Ward, her nephew, and Diane Lane, her secretary. Kildare makes a house call on Mrs. Stanford where he talks with her sister Amy about an argument they had over an Ouija board.

Amy believes that she is responsible for her sister's condition while Mrs. Stanford suffers a heart attack after seeing a ghost. The doctors sneak into the house later and discover Diane's scheme to pose as a ghost to get the $100,000 left her in Mrs. Stanford's will.

Guests: Peggy Webber, Lillian Buyeff, David Ellis and Isabel Randolph.

There are no details available on episodes 27 and 28

29. "Buffalo Barney McClure" August 10, 1950

McClure (Barton Yarbrough), a professional cowboy, is Blair's newest patient. When he meets Parker, McClure says she's his kind of woman.

The doctors find that McClure's dental bridge is lodged in his stomach but he refuses treatment. McClure later goes after Carew with his pistol, which is loaded with blanks, then later cheats Carew out of $260 in a game of Three Card Monte.

30. "Operation at Sea" August 17, 1950

A crewman on the SS Palermo needs an operation and Kildare determines during the radio call from the ship that the man needs an appendectomy. He discovers that the ship's radioman was once a Navy medic but he refuses to aid with the operation.

Kildare must go to the ship himself to perform the operation. Kildare says he'll talk with Gillespie about the operation.

Guests: Jack Webb, Raymond Burr, Jack Kruschen and Herb Ellis.

There are no details available on episodes 31 and 32

33. "Carew's Bad Day" September 7, 1950

A new patient is in a diabetic coma while Carew wants Kildare to guide a prospective donor's secretary around Blair General. However, Gillespie assigns Kildare to aid an intern with the new patient.

Carew discovers that Miss Mudd, who he thinks is the secretary, is actually the new state medical examiner when Guinion, the real secretary, arrives to see Carew. The doctors poke fun at Carew and Parker, whom Gillespie accuses of not having a brain. Gillespie says he has a plan to straighten out Carew's error.

Guests: Isabel Jewell, Will Wright and Wilms Herbert.

34. "Marion Lewis" September 14, 1950

Kildare tries to help Marion, a teenager with a drinking problem, despite Gillespie's warning against doing it. When her parents come to the hospital, they argue about Marion and Kildare refuses to release the girl.

Meanwhile, Sergeant Blaine calls to report that Marion is wanted for shoplifting. The doctors discuss Marion with her father, who talks about his own upbringing. After the Lewises decide to talk over what to do with Marion, Kildare releases her to their care.

Guests: Jack Kruschen, Lurene Tuttle, Tol Avery and Barbara Ruark.

35. "Sam Lubinski" September 21, 1950

Lubinski is injured when the rung of an iron ladder gets stuck in his stomach. Kildare goes to the site with Weyman to assist him since Lubinski is trapped in an underground tunnel.

Parker gets an operating room for Kildare and Gillespie. Weyman searches the tunnel to find the match of a fragment that lodged in Lubinski's spine. Kildare and a surgeon named Dave Radford operate on and cure Lubinski of the paralysis caused by the fragment.

Guests: Ed Max, Frank Gerstle, Byron Kane, Vic Perrin and Tudor Owen.

36. "Willie Mumpkin" September 28, 1950

Mumpkin's wife, Betty Jane, is expecting a baby and Kildare tries to calm him down. Meanwhile, Gillespie tries to pair Kildare with Diane Varner, a new staff nurse at Blair.

Mumpkin is worried that the couple will be given the wrong baby but Kildare says that almost never happens and the Mumpkins have a baby boy. Carew complains about Lumpkin's antics while Varner tells Gillespie she is engaged, but not to Kildare.

Guests: William Tracy, Sharon Douglas and Georgia Ellis.

There are no details available on episodes 37 and 38
The show moved to Fridays as of October 20, 1950.

39. "Eddie Jenkins" October 20, 1950

Jenkins is suspected of setting a fire at a pier during which a watchman died. Jenkins, who admits to suffering from headaches, says he heard a conversation among three men, one of whom had an accent.

Weyman is angered by how a man named Craig is treating Jenkins while Parker and Kildare try to find out what causes Eddie's headaches. Craig later supplies a tape which has the voice Eddie heard on it.

Weyman—who greets Kildare using the Bugs Bunny cartoon phrase "What's up, Doc?" —saves him from Maxen, the owner of a warehouse, during a fight when Maxen holds Kildare at gunpoint.

Guests: Raymond Burr, Whitfield Conner and Jerry Farber.

40. "Ling Co" October 23, 1950

Co, the grandfather of local restaurant owner Eddie Chen, is not well and has decided to die. Co allows Gillespie, an old friend of his, to examine him.

Co, injured in a car accident several years before, refuses treatment although both Gillespie and Kildare say it is necessary. Chen and Kildare concoct a plan to make Co agree to surgery but he doesn't fall for it.

Guests: Georgia Ellis, Paul Frees and Tudor Owen.

There are no details available on episodes 41 and 42

Note: The titles of episodes 43, "Mr. Bradley's Damaged Heart," and 44, "Mr. Kramer's Chronic Enteritis," were supplied by Jerry Haendiges' Vintage Radio Logs.

43. "Mr. Bradley's Damaged Heart" November 17, 1950

Bradley tells the doctors that he must finish a firm his project is working on in Mexico despite having a damaged heart. After witnessing another of Parker and Gillespie's arguments, Kildare tells Gillespie that Bradley is returning to the hospital.

Bradley agrees to a surgery and the doctors discuss why people ignore the warning signs their bodies give them. After the surgery, Bradley retires to a farm in Vermont.

Guests: Will Thurman and Vic Perrin.

44. "Mr. Kramer's Chronic Enteritis" November 24, 1950

Kildare suggests Parker take up a hobby to deal with how Gillespie treats her. The hobby is oil painting and Parker's first painting is called "The Operation."

When Parker is taken ill, she shows the same symptoms as Kramer. Kramer's illness is caused by his work while Parker's is caused by her hobby. When Parker returns to work, Gillespie tells her to go back to bed but compliments her on her painting. It wins an award in a contest.

Trivia: A snippet of Schumann's *Dragnet* theme is used in this episode. Ayres and Barrymore's first appearance of Kildare and Gillespie on radio was in the October 13, 1938 episode of "Good News of 1939" in an excerpt from the film *Young Dr. Kildare*.

45. "Lady Dunabee's Annual Visit" December 1, 1950.

Guests: Ed Max and Isabel Randolph

46. "Arthur Morgan" December 8, 1950

Morgan is injured in an accident and brought to Blair. Kildare had read a passage on brain surgery in a 200-year-old book he and Gillespie had found in a bookstore just before Morgan's accident.

Mrs. Morgan refuses to permit an operation despite Kildare's finding signs of a cerebral hemorrhage during an examination of Morgan. Carew tries to convince Mrs. Morgan of the need for surgery and fails but she does permit a spinal tap.

Parker pretends to be a patient in an attempt to convince Mrs. Morgan to agree to the operation. After the surgery, the Morgans make a present of the book Gillespie had been admiring in the store.

Guests: Vic Perrin, Lurene Tuttle and Georgia Ellis.

*** *There are no details available on episodes 47 and 48* ***

49. "David Norton" December 29, 1950

Norton, a youngster suffering from pneumonia, is the subject of a custody battle between his parents. The doctors discuss the situation with his governess, Miss Dilbert.

With Carew's unwilling support, Kildare plots to reunite the parents as David's temperature keeps going up. The Nortons give Carew a gift of maple sugar candy, but Gillespie keeps it for himself and Kildare.

Guests: Isabel Jewell, Stacy Harris, Jay Novello, Jeffrey Silver and Lynn Ainley.

50. "Nick Mazetti" January 5, 1951

The newspapers call Mazetti "The Payroll Bandit." Lt. Ed Dana comes to Blair with Mazetti, who is wounded during his most recent job. He assigns Sgt. Riley to guard Mazetti. He later takes Varner hostage, using Riley's gun.

Parker and Kildare treat the wounded Riley while Dana sets up roadblocks to trap him. However, he is in Blair's pathology lab and takes Kildare hostage there.

When Mazetti breaks a bottle in the lab, Kildare and Varner convince Mazetti that he's been exposed to leprosy even though the bottle only contained lanolin.

Guests: Barton Yarbrough, Barney Phillips and Vic Perrin.

51. "Dr. Gillespie's Testimonial Dinner" January 12, 1951

Kildare and Parker keep the dinner a secret from Gillespie, who thinks the hospital board wants him to retire. Carew and Kildare talk about Gillespie's recent behavior while Weyman and Gillespie go out bowling.

Gillespie later pretends to be ill and Kildare convinces Carew to move the dinner to another day. While going over medical reports, Kildare and Varner discuss their relationship. Gillespie considers making Weyman his assistant.

Guest: Ed Max.

52. "Dr. Conlon" January 19, 1951

Gillespie and Kildare devise a plan to expose Conlon as a quack with Gillespie posing as Kildare's father. Carew forbids Kildare from taking any action after Parker tells him about the plan. However, the doctors discover that Conlon himself is ill and will die within a year without treatment for his cancer.

Kildare tells Conlon he's out of business after he gives a treatment to Gillespie. Kildare says he'll help Conlon if he confesses to his actions. Varner later tells Kildare that he forgot about a date with her.

Guests: Ed Max, Sarah Selby and Raymond Burr.

53. "Joe Finley" January 26, 1951

Finley, who's only twenty-four, is suffering from a gastric ulcer, and his foreman, Barney Schumann, tells the doctors that Finley is suspected of embezzling from his firm.

The doctors discover that Mrs. Finley, who is bedridden with acute anemia, and that she is being treated by a "Dr." Blackthorne with aid from Schumann. Blackthorne is sentenced to 10 years in prison for his actions.

Joel Bigelow took over as the show's director with this episode, which was written by E. Jack Neumann and John Michael Hayes.

Guests: Paul Dubov, Isabel Jewell, Paul Frees, Anne Diamond and Jay Novello.

54. "Oliver Van Meter" February 2, 1951

Kildare has to cancel another date with Varner when Carew assigns him Van Meter's case. The man suffers from an allergy which runs from Monday to Friday every week.

The doctors take a case history from Van Meter and Kildare has him transferred to a hospital outside New York City. Carew later tracks the doctors to their favorite restaurant where he says he received a night letter from Van Meter saying that he is sick again.

They discover that Van Meter's allergy was caused by ink in his Sunday newspaper while Gillespie, who had a similar problem, is allergic to cats.

Writer: Paul Franklin.

Guests: Wilms Herbert and Margie Liszt.

55. "John Bremerton" February 9, 1951

Gillespie thinks that Bremerton's hand ulceration is caused by undulant fever but Kildare disagrees with the diagnosis. Jed, a wilderness guide, tells Kildare that he thinks Bremerton's condition was caused by a bear he caught and skinned.

Kildare brings the bear to the hospital, an action that Carew questions. Later, Bremerton's father, who is a neurosurgeon, takes over the case.

Bremerton later joins some Blair staff, including Kildare, at Jed's farm where some of his livestock is dying. With the aid of a crew of veterinarians, they treat the animals for anthrax and Bremerton returns his son to Kildare's care.

Writer: Joel Murcott.

Guests: Will Wright, Tom Holland and Theodore von Eltz. Bob Anderson took over Dick Joy's place as announcer as of this episode.

56. "Pete Cosloff" February 16, 1951

Kildare volunteers to see if Cosloff, who has wounded Captain Daggett, is holding any hostages. Daggett doesn't like the idea but sees no other solution and while Kildare is talking with Cosloff, Gillespie is finding out when he came to the United States.

Cosloff is holding a boy hostage just before Parker says Carew is looking for the doctors. Cosloff was in a concentration camp and is confusing the past and present. Kildare gets the gun Cosloff is using away from him and his treatment.

Writer: Joel Murcott.

Guests: Ted de Corsia and Lawrence Dobkin.

57. "Buck Houston" February 23, 1951

Houston, a cowboy star, is suffering from a back problem and Carew tells the doctors to treat him. X-rays reveal Houston is not injured and the problem is psychosomatic.

Kildare takes Houston to the children's ward where he and the children are aided as Houston makes a donation to help remodel the ward.

Writer: Paul Franklin.

Guests: Barton Yarbrough, Johnny McGovern and Mary McGovern.

58. "David Cooper" March 2, 1951

Cooper, who is recovering from injuries suffered in a plane crash, smashes a mirror when he sees his face after Kildare removes the bandages from it. Meanwhile, Parker is again upset by the way Gillespie treats her.

The doctors find Mrs. Cooper in her home on Long Island where she tells them that she is filing for divorce. Kildare blames himself when Cooper tries to commit suicide and thinks he will try again.

Cooper finally agrees to accept the help of Sinclair, a plastic surgeon, while Gillespie uses Parker to duck a confrontation with Carew. The doctors make plans to go golfing.

Writers: E. Jack Neumann and John Michael Hayes.

Guests: Lawrence Dobkin, Yvonne Peattie and Isabel Jewell.

Medical note: Kildare begins calling Gillespie "Dr. G" in this episode.

59. "Edward Carlton" March 9, 1951

Gillespie believes that Carlton, the victim of a dog bite, is suffering from rabies. Mrs. Carlton tells the doctors that she believes her husband was bitten by a dog named Spot. Weyman and Kildare find the dog and discover it is owned by a neighbor child named Bobby.

Weyman and Kildare hide the dog while Carlton's condition gets worse. Kildare believes that Mrs. Carlton is influencing her son while his medical history reveals that he has a history of asthma caused by dogs. The doctors take Spot back to Bobby and replace the bike he sold to get money for Spot's treatment.

Writer: Joel Murcott.

Guests: Ed Max, Jeffrey Silver, Vic Perrin and Isabel Randolph.

60. "Amy Dickens" March 16, 1951

Dickens is working on a book when Kildare comes to examine her broken leg and outlines a program of treatment. Her new boyfriend, Paul Campbell, the driver of the car in which Amy was injured, comes to see her.

She refuses treatment and her condition gets worse. Kildare believes that if her publisher, Lloyd Emerson, expressed interest in her novel that it would help her. Meanwhile, Parker and Gillespie argue about whom should retire first.

Emerson gives both Paul and Amy jobs, saying that with the proper training, Amy would be a fine writer.

Writers: E. Jack Neumann and John Michael Hayes.

Guests: William Bakewell, Peggy Webber and Earle Ross.

61. "Cathy Morton" March 23, 1951

Kildare agrees to see the baby of Cathy Morton (nee Winslow) since he knew Cathy when she was a child. Gillespie becomes fond of the baby which Cathy wants to put up for adoption since her husband (who is in the Marines) doesn't know about the child.

The Mortons are separated and Kildare reluctantly agrees to arrange the adoption. In a plan hatched by Gillespie, Parker and Carew pose as an Australian couple who want to adopt the baby. The couple reconciles after Cathy reacts to the plan the way Gillespie intended.

Writer: Joel Murcott.

Guests: Vic Perrin, Jack Kruschen and Isabel Jewell.

62. "Joan Quinn" March 30, 1951

Quinn replaces Verner while she is on vacation. When this leads to Kildare and Quinn becoming involved. Gillespie and Byrd get Carew's aid in having Quinn transferred to the orthopedics ward. This results in Kildare confronting Carew and Gillespie, then Gillespie arguing with Parker.

Gillespie and Weyman see Kildare carrying some books from his office and think he is planning to leave. Shortly afterwards, Gillespie collapses and Kildare orders a series of tests run on him. He then tells Gillespie that Quinn is married to a friend of his.

Writers: E. Jack Neumann and John Michael Hayes.

Guests: Ed Max, Eleanor Audley and Betty Lou Gerson.

63. "Gillespie's New Suit" April 6, 1951

Kildare gives Gillespie a physical and the doctors discuss the possibility of his having an eye ailment. Gillespie admits to working on a paper for a conference to be held the following week.

Kildare and Parker discuss Gillespie's needing a new suit and devise a plan to let him think it is his own idea. When Gillespie discovers the role patient Suzan Deschon played in the plan, he refuses to wear the new suit. It results in his being named the best-dressed doctor at the meeting.

Writer: Joel Murcott.

Guests: Ann Diamond and Julius Matthews.

64. "Yukon Joe Moran" April 13, 1951

Gillespie thinks Moran, who's about to be discharged, is a phony. Moran is telling Carew and Parker about his success as a prospector while the doctors observe Parker's interest in him.

The doctors discover that Carew and Parker have both bought shares in Moran's gold mine, then investigate the matter. They trail him to a hotel where they discover that he plans on going to Florida with his victims' money. The doctors then devise a plan to outsmart Moran with help from a local newspaper.

Writer: Joel Murcott.

Guest: Peter Leeds.

There are no details available on episodes 65 through 68

69. "Mysterious Hemophiliac Patient" May 18, 1951

A patient using the name of John Smith is actually King Phillip III, the patient of the title. Parker and the doctors discover through a series of tests that the king is also suffering from cancer.

The king, who wants to live until his nation becomes a democracy, accepts Kildare's suggestion to undergo surgery. Sarvo, Phillip's bodyguard, donates blood for the surgery and is later elected his country's first president.

Writer: Joel Murcott.

Guests: Larry Dobkin and Ben Wright.

70. "Dr. Gillespie's New Office" May 25, 1951

The doctors and Parker try to get Gillespie's office remodeled although Kildare tells Carew that he thinks it's a bad idea. The plan to get it done involves having Gillespie go fishing at Carew's country home.

Gillespie, angered when he sees the new office, threatens to leave Blair. Even after Kildare (on orders from Carew) buys back Gillespie's old roll top desk for $50 at an auction, Gillespie is still intent on leaving Blair.

Kildare and Carew find a false bottom in one of the desk drawers, Beasley, the auctioneer, brings in what the false bottom concealed—a packet of letters that Gillespie wrote to Nurse Molly Byrd 40 years ago. Parker turns on the intercom so she, Carew and Kildare can eavesdrop on Gillespie and Byrd.

Writers: E. Jack Neumann and John Michael Hayes.

Guests: Betty Blythe.

There are no details available on episodes 71 and 72

73. "Pedro, Mariz and Rosie" June 15, 1951

Kildare gets sick while he and Gillespie are on vacation in the Arizona desert. They stop at a sanitarium operated by Dr. Simmons, an old friend. When Kildare recovers, he agrees to aid Pedro, a local resident, who needs help with his pet burro.

Kildare has a relapse and realizes he needs an appendectomy if he is going to survive. A storm causes a flash flood just as Gillespie is preparing to leave so he can help Kildare, who knows he'll have to operate on himself if help doesn't arrive soon. After the operation, performed by Gillespie, Kildare buys a new burro for them and they name it after him.

Writer: Joel Murcott.

Guests: Lillian Buyeff, Anthony Barrett and Wilms Herbert.

74. "Paul Bailey" June 22, 1951

Carew asks Kildare to substitute for Bailey, an intern who failed to report for ambulance duty. Carew schedules a special meeting of Blair's board about Bailey and he is suspended when he doesn't show up at the hearing.

The doctors are discussing Bailey's record when Parker tells them that Bailey is now a patient. Kildare discovers that Bailey has had a nervous breakdown. His landlady comes to see Bailey and says she is angry at the doctors. Gillespie devises a plan to get Bailey to return to medicine.

Writers: E. Jack Neumann and John Michael Hayes.

Guests: Gloria Gordon, Larry Dobkin and Ann Diamond.

There are no details available on episodes 75 and 76

77. "Walter Benton" July 13, 1951

Weyman is suspected of stealing $25,000 from Benton, a heart attack patient, shortly before his death, by Kramer, the police detective investigating the case. Carew and the doctors argue when Weyman is found with a ring Benton was wearing when he died.

Kildare talks with Bill Walsh, Benton's attorney, whom Benton's daughter Valerie says poisoned his mind against Valerie. When Kerner and Kildare talk with Valerie, she inadvertently confesses to murdering her father.

Writer: Joel Murcott.

Guests: Ed Max, Herb Ellis, Yvonne Peattie, Barney Phillips and Warren Zavenell.

78. "Evelyn Briggs" July 20, 1951

Briggs is a fellow guest at the resort where the doctors are fishing. Kildare discovers that she is suffering from diphtheria and tells Converse, the resort's owner, that the place must be quarantined. Constable Allison, the one-man police force in Wentworth, the nearest town, thinks the doctors are lying when Evelyn disappears.

Converse and Chuck Rivers, a gangster, drive the doctors to the local train station at gunpoint. Gillespie goes for help while Kildare searches for Evelyn. He's forced to give Rivers some of the diphtheria serum.

Writers: John Michael Hayes and E. Jack Neumann.

Guests: Peggy Webber, Wally Maher, Sheldon Leonard and Barton Yarbrough.

79. "Robert Lane" July 27, 1951

Carew wants to investigate the activities of Lane, an intern, and Gillespie wonders why Kildare didn't report Lane. Kildare warns Lane of Carew's investigation. The doctors and Weyman later search for Lane.

Weyman and Kildare discover that Lane has been illegally practicing medicine and stole a piece of equipment from the hospital. They find a notebook with a series of names, one of which is Lane's pregnant sister.

William P. Rousseau returned the direct the show's last two episodes, both of which were written by Les Crutchfield.

80. "Alice Bradley" August 3, 1951

The doctors try to help an amnesia victim regain her memory. A man claiming to be her father says her name is Alice Bradley.

Alice says the man is not her father and Carew tells the man that she should stay in the hospital. Parker blames herself when Alice disappears. Kildare and Weyman find the girl in a cemetery. Kildare then gets Bradley to read a letter from her Uncle George that explains what Alice found in her diary.

Guests: William Conrad, Lurene Tuttle, Ed Max and Marie Blake.

§

Raymond Massey and Richard Chamberlain.

Chapter 2

The First
TV Season
September 28, 1961
to May 24, 1962

T he show starred Richard Chamberlain as the title character with Raymond Massey as Dr. Gillespie. It ran on Thursdays at 8:30 p.m. (EST) for its first four seasons.

Among the semi-regulars during the first season were Ken Berry as Dr. John Kapish, Sam Reese as Dr. Dan Shanks, Jud Taylor as Dr. Tom Gerson, Eddie Ryder as Dr. Simon Agurski, Harvey Korman as Dr. B. R. Leibman, Gary Judis as Dr. Vincent Barnes, James Callahan as Dr. Yates Atkinson, Jean Inness as Nurse Beatrice Fain, Madge Blake as Nurse Helen Phipps, Maxine Stuart as Nurse Mary Ayers, Dan Tobin as Jones, Clegg Hoyt as Max and Joan Patrick as Susan Deigh.

During its first four seasons, *Kildare* ran just before *Hazel*, based on the *Saturday Evening Post* cartoons of Ted Key, who died in mid-2008. Its stars were Shirley Booth, Don DeFore and Whitney Blake.

1. "Twenty-Four Hours" September 28, 1961

Kildare's first patient as an intern as Julia Dressard (Beverly Garland). When Dr. Justin Montag, who is in charge of Blair General Hospital's Ward E, it leads to Kildare finding her drunk at Mac's where Mac asks for his help.

Despite Gillespie's advice to the contrary, Kildare becomes involved in Dressard's personal life and gets into a confrontation with Dressard's ex-husband (Robert Karnes).

Meanwhile Miss Deigh, Gillespie's receptionist, invites Kildare to a party.

After Dressard tries to commit suicide a second time, Kildare gets help from Dr. Solomon, an expert on alcoholism.

Writer: E. Jack Neumann. Neumann and Jean Holloway both wrote for The Story of Dr. Kildare radio series.

Director: Boris Sagal.

Also appearing: Jack Weston and Carol Rossen.

Episode notes: The F.A.C.P. behind Gillespie's name in the closing credits stood for Fellow of the American College of Physicians. Kildare's advice on how to solve problems from a fellow intern—women and liquor—probably don't make much sense today.

Trivia: The book *15,003 Answers* lists "24 Hours" as the premiere episode of *ER* on NBC. That show began its long run on September 19, 1994.

2. "Immunity" October 5, 1961

After Kildare and Fain examine a patient on whom they find lesions, Kildare discusses the case with Kapish and Agurski. Another intern, Anne Warner (Gail Kobe) tells Kildare that the patient is Polish and serves as his translator.

Kildare and Gillespie diagnose the man's illness as smallpox and this leads to Warner and Kildare going to a social hall in a Polish neighborhood where they vaccinate everyone. Kildare tries to find out why Warner has cut herself off from her own culture while the patient (whose name is Wolski) will only talk with Gillespie, whom he calls the old doctor.

Cox (William Fawcett), a transient who robbed Wolski, sees a newspaper headline about him. Wolski dies when he tries to escape. Warner tells them that Wolski thought the doctors were Nazis and begins to cry when they return to the Polish neighborhood.

Writer: Andy Lewis.

Director: Boris Sagal.

Ted Knight is also featured in this episode.

Episode note: The show's first kiss was shared by Chamberlain and Kobe.

3. "Shining Image" October 12, 1961

Julie Lawler (Suzanne Pleshette) is Kildare's newest patient. Not knowing what she is suffering from, Julie goes to see her brother Arthur Penmore (Edward Andrews) where she asks what's wrong with her.

After she has a confrontation with Kildare about her leukemia, Kildare tells Julie that she needs to finish something or at least try to. Penmore describes to Kildare how Julie has been treated all her life.

Julie talks with a priest about her illness, and then gives up on her projects, a sculpture and a play to go on a date with Bill Olsen. When she gets sick, Olsen takes her to Blair.

Writer: John T. Kelley.

Director: Buzz Kulik.

Trivia: John Fielder, another frequent *Kildare* guest and later a regular on *The Bob Newhart Show,* appears in this episode. The songs "Dr. Freud" and "Happy Days Are Here Again" are used.

4. "Winter Harvest" October 19, 1961

Kildare and Gillespie discuss Dr. Charles Dubro (Charles Bickford), a surgeon whose operations—in Kildare's opinion—take too long. Gillespie and Dr. Norman Hackett (Hayden Rorke), Blair's chief of surgery, discuss Dubro's performance.

Meanwhile, Kildare gets a new patient—hypochondriac Lorenzo Lawson (Gavin MacLeod). Agurski and Dr. Galdi (Sandy Kenyon) assist Dr. Dubro in operating on Rico, Blair's parking attendant, who passed out while driving Gillespie's car. It is Dubro's last surgery as he announces his retirement at his 35th anniversary party.

Writer: John T. Furia Jr.

Director: Lamont Johnson.

Episode notes: Dubro and Gillespie play both golf and pool during this episode. The song "For He's a Jolly Good Fellow" is used. Blair General Hospital is located in Los Angeles in this show while it was set in New York for the movie and radio series. Also appearing in this episode were Herschel Bernardi and Noam Pitlik.

This is how Gillespie would look on a casual Friday.

5. "The Million Dollar Property" October 26, 1961

Actress Kathy Stebbins (Anne Francis) is Kildare's newest patient. The Blair staff gossip about her while Gillespie talks with acting teacher Louisa Humber (Cathleen Nesbit) about Stebbins.

Part of Kathy's problems emanate from a group of hangers-on who call themselves The Pride of the Lions. Their leader is Kenny Hallerton (played by game show host Jan Murray).

Stebbins, who's fallen in love with Kildare, talks about giving up acting and doing something in medicine. She watches later as her friends make fun of Kildare. When Kildare returns to the hospital, Gillespie asks for his help on a project.

Writer: Ernest Kinoy

Director: Herbert Hirschhorn (the show's first producer).

Joby Baker is also featured in this episode.

6. "Admitting Service" November 2, 1961

Dr. Toby Cunningham (played by William Shatner, one of the actors Chamberlain beat out for the Kildare part) is Kildare's supervisor in the emergency room. They argue about whether to admit a patient named Parker. Later on, the interns discuss their social life or lack thereof.

When Kildare is assigned to ambulance duty, he discovers that Parker has died. Parker's sister, a Mrs. Fife, says she is authorizing an autopsy to determine the cause of death and that she plans to sue Blair General.

After Kildare tells Cunningham that he still disagrees with him about the Parker case, Cunningham tells his wife that Kildare is no longer their friend. Gillespie tells Kildare that Cunningham was right in the Parker case and then later addresses his staff about the difference between mistakes and malpractice.

Writer: E. Jack Neumann.

Director: Eliot Silverstein.

Also appearing in this episode were Gloria Talbott, Robert B. Williams, Amy Fields, Helena Nash, John Hart, Gertrude Flynn, Dick Crockett, Gary Hunley, Roy Sickner and Francisco Villalobos.

Episode notes: Gillespie cites the code of Hammurabi under which a surgeon's hands can be cut off if a patient dies. In a staff meeting, Gillespie says that anyone who wishes to smoke may do so.

7. "The Lonely Ones" November 9, 1961

When Kildare goes home to see his parents, Harry Benton (Dick York), an old friend of the family, asks Kildare to be the best man at his upcoming wedding. Benton tells Kildare how he and his fiancée Martha met.

Martha's mother later calls Kildare and they discover that Martha has locked herself in her room. Kildare breaks down the door, and then argues with Martha and later finds a bottle of pills in her medicine cabinet.

Benton and Kildare later find Martha at Paul's Motel where she is unconscious from a drug overdose. When she is taken to Blair, Gillespie talks with

Martha about her addiction, Gillespie says it will take work on both her and the hospital's part to affect a cure.

Writers: John Knuebuhl and Archie L. Tegland

Director: John Brahm

Episode note: Robert B. Leib, a semi-regular on *Hazel*, plays Dr. Stephen Kildare in this episode. Also appearing were Howard Caine, Carolyn Kearney, Ford Rainey and Katherine Squire.

8. "Holiday Weekend" November 16, 1961

Dr. Paul Willis (Dick Sargent) is one of Blair's few doctors to get the holiday off. He borrows Kildare's car to pick up his father (Dabbs Greer) and is injured in an accident.

Ben Laney (Edward Binns), the other driver, says the accident was not his fault while a surgical team works on Willis' heart and liver. The senior Willis confronts Laney after hearing a policeman asking Kildare about the accident.

Gillespie orders Dr. Willis put in an oxygen tent when a lab test shows that he is suffering from staph pneumonia. Willis later becomes one of the 400 people to die during the holiday weekend.

Writer: Alvin Boretz.

Director: Gerald Mayer.

Also appearing were John Marley, Lew Gallo, Donald Randolph and Pamela Duncan.

Episode note: By a weird coincidence, *Bewitched*'s two Darrins guest star in successive episodes of this series.

9. "The Patient" November 23, 1961

An accident makes Kildare a patient on Blair's Ward D. Kelsey, one of his fellow patients, tells Kildare that the accident could paralyze him and Kildare bawls out Miss Novotny, the nurse's aide whose negligence caused the accident.

Kapish visits Kildare and finds himself having to examine Mrs. Kelsey. Kildare wakes the following morning to find his fellow patients want him moved from Ward D.

Kildare asks Gerson if he can see his X-rays while the ward's other patients can't eat because of their worry over Stedman, another patient. When Kildare is released, he is examined by Gerson and Laughlin, another staff doctor.

Medical note: During his stint as a patient, Kildare finds himself getting a sponge bath under the supervision of Miss Whitney (Jean Stapleton in her only appearance on *Dr. Kildare*.)

Writer: Archie L. Tegland.

Director: Eliot Silverstein.

Also appearing in this episode were Guy Raymond, Frank Killmond, Mark Allen and Vaughn Taylor as Ward D patients; Noah Keen, Jenny Maxwell, William Swan, Tom Troupe and Josie Lloyd.

Trivia: During the "Little Ricky Learns to Play the Drums" episode of *I Love Lucy,* Ricky tells Lucy to return a junior Dr. Kildare kit that she bought for Little Ricky.

The musical score for this episode was composed by Carmen Dragon, while the show's theme was composed by Jerry Goldsmith. A vocal version done by Chamberlain reached No. 10 on many record charts.

10. "For the Living" November 30, 1961

Ben Rainey is in a coma after an accident at his home and according to Gillespie, he may be so indefinitely. Ben's brother Fred (Charles McGraw) comes home to aid the family while his wife Pamela (Beatrice Straight) stays by his bedside.

Dr. Mason tells Fred that his brother might never regain consciousness but still could outlive him. Fred tries to convince Pamela to place Ben in a sanitarium, then gives Ben his nightly shot or says he did.

Kildare is called to the Rainey home after Ben's death and gives Pamela a sedative. Tommy finds out what happened and thinks his mother did it. When Gillespie finds out what Fred did, Fred asks why Gillespie didn't do it himself.

Writers: Jerome Ross, John T. Kelley and John Dunkel.

Director: Elliott Silverstein.

Also featured in this episode were Tom Greenway, Peter Helm and Ann Shoemaker. McGraw would assume the semi-regular role of Dr. Hasker later in the show's run.

Trivia: A similar story about mercy killing, "Bridge of Mercy" appeared on March 5, 1939 during the first season of the *Screen Guild Theater* radio series. It starred Paul Muni, Josephine Hutchinson and Lionel Atwill. George Cukor directed the play.

11. "Second Chance" December 7, 1961

Kildare is concerned about Bill Mitchell (Ross Martin), a fellow intern who is suffering from fatigue. He suspects Mitchell may be suffering from myasthenia gravis and Gillespie orders a series of tests run.

Anne Garner (Ellen MacRae, later Ellen Burstyn) admits to Kildare that she is scared of illness. Meanwhile, Kildare has a confrontation with Dr. Zachary Hardy over the care of Cathy Ashmond, another patient.

Mitchell has another attack after an argument with Anne. Gillespie says that Mitchell can still be a doctor. Mitchell and Anne reconcile.

Writers: John Blake, Jan Winters and Eve Ettinger.

Director: Buzz Kulik.

Barry Gordon, Donna Douglas, Justice Watson, Warren Kemmerling, Barbara Beaird and Rita Lynn also appeared in this episode. Douglas would land her most famous role, that of Elly Mae Clampett in *The Beverly Hillbillies,* in the 1962-63 TV season.

12. "Hit and Run" December 14, 1961

Jamie Carroll (Roger Mobley) is injured when the car driven by his father Fred (Richard Kiley) is struck in a hit-and-run accident. Paul Adams (Dick Foran), a family friend, asks Jamie how he is before an ambulance takes him to Blair where Kildare is assigned to the case.

Immediate surgery is needed because Jamie's right arm is paralyzed. Tommy Adams, Jamie's friend, offers to donate blood for his friend's operation. Paul Adams says he'll try to find Carroll and get his authorization for an operation but Carroll has disappeared, disguising himself as a doctor.

Gillespie gets Judge Isley to authorize the operation while Kildare tracks Carroll to the Blair lab. Carroll surrenders after talking with Kildare and Adams.

Writers: Louis Peterson and Norman Katkov.

Director: Alexander Singer.

Also appearing in this episode were Michael McGreevey, Paul Bryar and Helen Wallace.

Trivia: The musical score for most episodes was provided by Harry Sukman.

13. "Season to Be Jolly" December 21, 1961

Jones, the hospital's new PR man, is taking Christmas pictures around the hospital and follows Kildare when a man dressed as Santa Claus is admitted. Kildare has an argument with "Santa" as a group of children watches. Gillespie and Kildare then try to get information from their new patient.

In the cafeteria, Gillespie (whose going on vacation is the subject of a hospital pool) joins Kildare, Agurski and Kapish for a cup of coffee. Meanwhile, Jones is trying to get a picture of "Santa" (Dan O'Herlihy). Hospital chaplain Paul Armstrong recognizes him as former minister Mark Addison.

Bishop Fanning later tells Gillespie about Addison's history while two new patients—Charlie (who gets sick every Christmas) and a pregnant woman—are admitted. Jones needs a picture of a newborn baby and Gillespie delivers the baby in a hospital elevator. The student nurses sing for the children in the pediatrics ward and Kildare reads them the Christmas story.

Writer: Jean Holloway.

Director: Elliott Silverstein.

Also appearing in this episode were Hayden Rorke, Kenneth MacKenna, Phil Arnold, William Fawcett, Bert Remsen and Meg Wyllie.

Episode Note: Kildare sings "Deck the Halls" while the student nurses sing "Jingle Bells," "O Holy Night," "It Came Upon a Midnight Clear" and "Joy to the World."

14. "Johnny Temple" December 28, 1961

Kildare treats Temple, a stabbing victim, who says he had just picked up some medicine just before he was assaulted. Kildare examines Temple the following morning after talking with his parents (Peter Whitney, Virginia Gregg).

When Kildare finds Johnny with a knife, he recommends the young man's transfer to the psychiatric ward, and unit director Dr. David Goldman recommends Johnny's immediate commitment after talking with him.

*15. "My Brother, the Doctor" January 4, 1962

In the only episode to focus on him, Dr. Simon Agurski (Eddie Ryder) tells his brother Nathan (Herschel Bernardi), an accountant, that he no longer needs help financing his medical education. Also featured in the episode are Alex Gerry, Mary LaRoche and Penny Santon.

Writers: Bruce Geller and Archie L. Tegland.

Director: Boris Sagal.

16. "The Administrator" January 11, 1962

Charles Ladovan (Joseph Cotten) has replaced Dr. Carew as Blair's administrator. He talks with Kildare while his wife (Dorothy Malone) visits with Gillespie. The Ladovans later discuss a party they are holding that night.

At the party, Blair board member Bill Rebere (Edmon Ryan) confronts Ladovan about the firing of a friend. Kildare overhears a conversation Rebere has later with Mrs. Ladovan.

Steven Devitt (Edgar Buchanan), another board member talks with Gillespie, about Ladovan's future at the hospital. Ladovan resigns the post and although the board votes to keep him on, the Ladovans say they're leaving Los Angeles.

Writer: Andy Lewis.

Director: Paul Stanley.

Stafford Repp was also featured in this episode.

Trivia: Dr. Carew was played by Ted Osborne on *The Story of Dr. Kildare* radio series.

*17. "Oh, My Daughter" January 25, 1962

Gillespie's pregnant daughter (Dina Merrill) attempts suicide. Victor Jory also appears in this episode, which was written by Betty Andrews and directed by Buzz Kulik.

*18. "The Search" February 1, 1962

Kulik also directed this episode in which a search is launched to find the source of a series of food poisoning cases. John Furia Jr. wrote the episode which had Jeremy Slate and Pippa Scott as its guest stars.

19. "The Glory Hunter" February 8, 1962

Dr. Tony Stuart (Alfred Ryder), director of a hospital in India, is welcomed to Blair while the press questions Mrs. Stuart (Miriam Colon), a native of that country, about health conditions there. Part of the reason for Stuart's trip is to accept an award.

During his examination of Stuart, the doctor tells Kildare about his right arm troubling him. During rounds, Gillespie questions Kapish about his treatment of a patient. Reporter Ned Lacey (Martin Balsam) calls Stuart a glory hound while he and Kildare are watching Mrs. Stuart's TV appearance at Mac's.

Stuart needs an operation and on a telethon, he announces Kildare as his successor. This starts donations of $500 or more rolling in and Lacey later confronts Stuart about his lying about his health.

Writers: John T. Kelley and Gerry Day.

Director: Lamont Johnson.

Also appearing in this episode were Cliff Norton, Ben Wright, Arte Johnson, Casey Adams and Connie Sawyer.

Martin Balsam and Angela Lansbury in *The Eleventh Hour* **episode "Something Crazy's Going On In the Back Room."**

20. "The Dragon" February 15, 1962

Mrs. Fain finds her husband (Jack Albertson), who has been gone for years, waiting for her when she comes home from work. When Gillespie and Mrs. Fain talk about her husband's return, she asks Gillespie to give him a job.

Meanwhile, Kildare is trying to help a patient who can't speak English. When Dr. Moore, another Blair staffer (Scott Marlowe) accidentally overdoses a patient, he has Lori Palmer (Margaret O'Brien), a nurse with whom he's involved, help him to cover up the incident.

When Gillespie discovers what happened, he makes Moore read Maimonides' Prayer for the Physician. Gillespie then says he'll recommend that Moore be dropped as an intern to the hospital board. Nurse Palmer later turns down Moore's marriage proposal while Fain again leaves his wife.

Writer: Andy Lewis.

Director: Robert Ellis Miller.

Elizabeth Perry and John Bliefer also appeared in this episode.

21. "The Stepping Stone" February 22, 1962

Gillespie recognizes a patient as Dr. Max Keller (Joseph Schildkraut), an old friend now engaged in research. He is suffering from malnutrition. Meanwhile, Dr. Art Bedlow (Roger Perry) tries to convince Keller's roommate Angelo Delvecchio (Eduardo Ciannelli) to authorize a post mortem if he doesn't survive an operation.

Kildare offers to aid Keller in his research after Keller's landlady, Mrs. Talmage, comes to see him. Gillespie and Agurski also become involved in helping. Keller and Gillespie are both widowers.

Bedlow calls Keller a has-been after Delvecchio says he will talk only to his former roommate. Delvecchio signs the form and gives it to Keller. Kildare and Bedlow come to see Keller in his basement lab in Mrs. Talmage's building. Keller insists on running lab tests on Bedlow before he gives him Delvecchio's consent form.

Writers: Archie L. and Janet L. Tegland.

Director: Elliot Silverstein.

Dorothy Konrad was also featured in the episode.

Trivia: Perry would appear as Dr. Edward White in a 1962 episode of *The Eleventh Hour.*

22. "The Bronc Buster" March 1, 1962

Kildare's cousin, Lucky Elcott (Arch Johnson), a rodeo rider, brings his son Buddy to Blair for an appendectomy. Kildare and Mary Reese, a hospital social worker, talk with Lucky about his arthritis and when Elcott comes to see his son, Kildare suggests that he get a regular job.

The doctors go to the rodeo with Miss Reese and watch as Elcott gets disqualified in the bareback riding. Two of Kildare's colleagues help him find Lucky jobs but neither one works out and Elcott goes back to the rodeo.

Kapish comes back from vacation and says he saw the Elcotts as they left the hospital. Kildare proudly tells his colleague that Elcott is his cousin.

Writer: Pat Fielder.

Director: Paul Stanley.

Also appearing in this episode were Billy Mumy, Hope Summers and Nancy Marshall.

Trivia: An arm wrestling match is featured while Gerson kisses Nurse Johnson in this episode. The songs "Home on the Range," "You Are My Lucky Star" and "Red River Valley" are included in the episode score.

*23. "Witch Doctor" March 8, 1962

Gillespie and Kildare battle a quack doctor (Pat Hingle) for the fate of a critically ill young woman (Joan Hackett). Lew Gallo and William Schallert are also featured in this episode, which was written by Alvin Boretz and directed by Lamont Johnson.

24. "The Roaring Boy-O" March 15, 1962

Kapish and Kildare bring poet John McHenry (Dan O'Herlihy in his second guest appearance this season) to Blair after he gets into a fight at Mac's. Kildare asks McHenry's friend, Sally Winters (Fay Spain) about his background.

Kildare and Mrs. Fain both suggest Winters go home while McHenry plots to escape from the hospital, but is stopped by Kildare and Kapish. When he does escape, Kildare and Winters track him to Mac's. McHenry, who is suffering from cirrhosis of the liver, flees to a church and claims sanctuary, then talks with a priest.

Gillespie confronts McHenry, telling him he may have only six months to live, while Kildare argues with him about his treatment of Winters. McHenry tells Winters to go home until he can function again and tells her that will probably be in six months.

Writers: John Whedon and Emmet Lovery.

Director: Elliot Silverstein.

25. "Solomon's Choice" March 29, 1962

Two women, Kitty Scola and Winona Pines (Barbara Baxley and Collin Wilcox) have babies at the same time while Kildare and Atkinson are working in obstetrics. The Scola baby dies while Mrs. Pines doesn't want her baby. Gillespie tells Kitty that she can return to work.

Kildare and Scola (William Schallert) talk with Kitty about adopting the Pines baby while the Pines have an argument and Jerome Pine tells his wife that he wants a divorce. Although Winona initially agrees to give up her baby, she later changes her mind.

The two women later have an argument over what's best for the baby.

Writers: John Furia Jr. and Anthony Lawrence.

Director: Lamont Johnson.

26. "A Very Present Help" April 5, 1962

Kildare's newest patients are Janet Parker (Patricia Crowley), who refuses to have an operation, and Sister Brigid Marie (Glynis Johns), who is facing surgery for gallstones. Gillespie suggests that the two women be roommates.

When they argue, Mrs. Parker tries to leave the hospital. Meanwhile, Kapish and Gerson are watching a medical show. The doctors then discuss Sister Brigid Marie and her effect on the hospital.

Kildare and Sister Brigid Marie later prevent Mrs. Parker from committing suicide. Gillespie and Bernie, representing Sister Brigid Marie's young clients, visit her just before her surgery.

Writer: John T. Dugan.

Director: Robert Butler.

Also appearing in this episode were Lew Gallo, Susan Petrone, Helen Wallace, Russell Thorson, Charity Grace, Bill Leslie, James Maloney, Nora Marlowe, Darlene Gillespie, Helen Clark and Donald Long.

27. "One for the Road" April 12, 1962

Kildare and Ayers are assigned to the new alcoholic ward being run by Dr. Paul Probeck (Lee Marvin), who tells Kildare his own story. One of the ward's patients is a John Doe (Paul Carr), who refuses to give any information about himself.

Doe is confronted by Kildare after he starts a fight in the ward. Probeck refuses to have Doe removed despite Gillespie ordering it. Grady (Charles Aidman), another patient on the ward, reports getting a job while Doe provokes Henderson to leave the ward.

When Grady and Doe are late getting back from passes, Kildare follows Probeck to a bar where he prevents Probeck from taking a drink.

Writers: Yale Peter Harrison and Robert Dozier.

Director: John Brahm.

Guests: Cliff Osmond, William Mims and Paul Gardner.

28. "The Horn of Plenty" April 19, 1962

Dr. Harry Nelson (Lloyd Bochner) orders bed rest for George Prentiss (Philip Bourneuf), one of his wealthy patients. Meanwhile, Kildare is tending to Frank Chernak, another patient, when he assigned to Prentiss.

Gillespie and Kildare discuss Nelson's conduct and Kildare's response to it with Gillespie suggesting Kildare apologize to Nelson. Nelson invites Kildare and Agurski to a party at his home.

At the party, Kildare meets Prentiss' daughter Joan (Elen Willard). Later, he talks with Chernak about his needing surgery for an ulcer. During a trip to the beach, Kildare and Joan discuss her past, including her mother's suicide.

Kildare later tells Joan that interns are only paid $60 a month. Kildare then has a meeting with Mrs. Nelson (Julie Adams) during which she talks about her past. Later, Joan breaks up with Kildare.

Writer: James Blumgarten.

Director: Paul Wendkos.

Also appearing: Sandy Kenyon, Steven Geray, Raymond Bailey and Charles Alvin Bell.

Trivia: Parts of this episode were filmed at Carillo State Park.

29. "The Chemistry of Anger" April 26, 1962

Kildare argues with Dr. Nick Keefe (Rip Torn), who's up for the post of Blair's chief resident, over his treatment of a pneumonia patient. The interns and nurses throw a party when Keefe doesn't get the job.

Keefe's treatment of Collins, another patient, causes another argument before Keefe and Kildare. Meanwhile, Gillespie decides to recommend Keefe for a job in Chicago.

Kildare and Gillespie work on Collins when he goes into convulsions a second time. They then discuss the case and Kildare says he thinks that Keefe should have gotten the chief residency post.

Writers: Dr. Marshall Goldberg and Jerry McNeely.

Director: William Graham.

Joyce Van Patten, Bert Remsen, Frederic Downs, Doris Kemper, Richard Benjamin and Elizabeth MacRae also appeared in this episode.

30. "Something of Importance" May 3, 1962

Kildare and Dr. Arthur Staples (Ivan Dixon) are assigned to work with Dr. Charles Hodiak (George Voskovec), a friend of Gillespie's who has been doing research on sickle cell anemia for 17 years. Agurski introduces Kildare to Dr. Barbara James, a victim of the disease.

When the doctors discover a treatment for the illness through animal testing, Gillespie says clinical testing could begin at Blair with Dr. James as a subject. Kildare and Hodiak argue about the study results and Kildare is dismissed from the project. Gillespie later talks with Kildare, who suspects Hodiak has been falsifying data. Before he resigns, Hodiak reveals what he did to Gillespie.

Writer: Sy Salkowitz.

Director: Elliot Silverstein.

Other guests in the episode were Frances Foster, Jack Doner, Adrienne Marden, Norman Kotcher and Ed Prentiss.

Trivia: There is a photo of a dog on Gillespie's desk. Whether said canine was named Hippocrates is unknown.

31. "A Distant Thunder" May 10, 1962

Kildare's newest patient is Lt. General John Sparrow (Dean Jagger), who's brought to Blair after causing a disturbance at a shooting gallery. Gillespie and Dr. Ernest Miller (Michael Constantine) discuss Sparrow's case with Miller saying that he believes Sparrow will eventually attempt suicide.

After Sparrow is placed on Gillespie's private service, he analyzes Kildare's character. Mrs. Amelia Lee (Nellie Burt), a volunteer, tries to give Sparrow a model rocket but Kildare makes her leave. When Sparrow later insults Mrs. Lee, Kildare confronts him.

Mrs. Lee later confronts Sparrow herself after watching Kildare and Sparrow debate the meaning of life. Sparrow, disguised as a doctor, goes to see Harold Lee and offers to help Mrs. Lee after Harold dies.

Writer: Gene Roddenberry (his *Star Trek* would inherit the *Kildare* time slot in 1966).

Director: Paul Wendkos.

Also appearing in this episode were Lizabeth Hush, Alexander Lockwood and Robert Winston.

32. "The Road to the Heart" May 17, 1962

Kildare agrees to cover for Kapish in admitting and finds Agurski sleeping on a gurney just before an ambulance brings in a patient. Kildare and Agurski try to discover what happened to the new patient, whose name is Tad Thornley.

Kildare talks with Tad's mother Elizabeth (Joanne Linville) about her son's condition. Agurski finds a rat poison container at the Thornley home and calls to see if there's an antidote. Gillespie comes in to supervise the case and the doctor discovers that Tad is deaf.

Mrs. Phipps tells Kildare to get some rest and calls Kildare when Tad begins having convulsions. Tad is moved to the children's ward where Kildare and Mrs. Phipps discover that he can hear. Gillespie confronts Kildare about his actions, than talks with Mrs. Thornley about an operation for Tad.

When Tad runs away from his mother in a drugstore, she calls Gillespie for help. A barking dog leads a milkman to the missing boy. Mrs. Thornley authorizes the operation after which the doctors test Tad's hearing.

Writers: Theodore and Mathilde Ferro, Jean Holloway.

Director: Elliot Silverstein.

Other guests in this episode were Rory O'Brien, Ed Prentiss, Della Sharman, Dorothy Neumann, John Dennis and Wilson Wood.

33. "Operation: Lazarus" May 24, 1962

Kildare discovers that one of the possible candidates for the testing of a new psychiatric drug is Dr. Carl Lantzinge (Sidney Blackmer), an old friend of his father. When Freddie tries to play ping pong with an unresponive Freddie Binns (Steve Franken), he talks with Dr. White (Bert Freed) about Binns and the other patients.

Mrs. Lantzinge (Mary Astor) confronts Gillespie about the study, which is being done at six hospitals including Blair. She and her lover Adam Ross meet while White is conducting a therapy session.

Kildare takes Lantzinge on a tour of the orthopedics ward, hoping to spark his memory since orthopedics was his specialty and Gillespie plays a game of chess with him. The doctors tell Mrs. Lantzinge that her husband's condition is improving and she tells them about the various treatments her husband has received.

Writer: Betty Andrews.

Director: Boris Sagal.

Ina Victor, Lauren Gilbert and Jean Allison also appeared in this episode, which closed the show's first season.

§

Richard Chamberlain and Yvette Mimeux in "Tyger, Tyger."

Chapter 3

The Second
TV Season
September 27, 1962
to June 6, 1963

J oining the cast were Lee Meriwether as Nurse Bonnie Tynes, Ruth McDevitt as Nurse Adele Fromm and Claudia Bryar as Nurse Maggie Simpson.

34. "Gravida One" September 27, 1962

Kildare, now assigned to the OB-GYN unit, talks with Doris Manning (Patricia Barry), who's having her first baby. Meanwhile, Gillespie's newest patient is Louis Conrad, an old friend who helped build Blair. He's suffering from an ulcer.

When Kildare and Dr. Stanley Shoates discuss the Manning case, Shoates says that a C-section is necessary. Conrad dies suddenly while Mrs. Manning, who keeps saying that she doesn't want a baby, has it.

Writer: E. Jack Neumann.
Director: Elliot Silverstein.

35. "The Burning Sky" October 4, 1962

Kildare and medical student Mark Hadley (Robert Redford) are dispatched as a medical team to a forest being consumed by wildfire. The fire covers 40,000 acres, according to Roy Drummond (Carroll O'Connor) of the Forest Service.

A little girl named Ellen Gates is their first patient. Kildare cares for her while Drummond takes Hadley to care for patients in the field. The doctors lose a patient, a firefighter who does of pulmonary edema.

Gillespie treats Norris (David Sheiner), a burn victim at Blair and finds that his carelessness started the fire. Hadley tells Kildare that he wants to go into research because he's afraid of seeing people die.

Kildare and Hadley have to operate on Ellen when Drummond tells them there's no way to get the little girl to the hospital before morning.

Writer: Ken Kolb.

Director: Lamont Johnson.

Trivia: The Los Angeles County Fire Department furnished film footage while the U.S. Forest Service aided in filming this episode.

36. "The Visitors" October 11, 1962

When suddenly taken ill, Makim Saund (John Cassavettes) is brought to Blair. Kildare tells Makim's father (Abraham Sofaer) that neurosurgery may be necessary as Saund has a brain tumor that could kill him.

Kildare also has a patient named Vernon Hackett (John Anderson), who lost his right leg in Korea. Makim asks Kildare to take him on a tour of Blair during which he meets Hackett and is then badgered by the press.

Makim and Kildare argue about the need for the operation but finally agree after having talks with Hackett and his wife (Patricia Houston). Dr. Coneely, a Blair staffer (David Lewis) tries to get Mahmel Homatha (Theodore Bikel), a fellow physician and a countryman of Saund, to act as a consultant but he refuses.

Gillespie says Homatha is not really a doctor because he put his interests and not the patient's first. As the Hacketts watch, Homatha lies about his role in Makim's operation.

This episode was written by Frank R. Pierson and directed by Paul Wendkos.

37. "The Mask Makers" October 18, 1962

Kildare, who is assigned to plastic surgery, talks with his friend Evy Schuler (Carolyn Jones) about her wanting an operation on her nose. After Kildare shows Evy some masks, she meets with Gillespie.

After the operation, Evy wonders about its effect on her. Dr. Larry Phelan (Mike Kellin) asks her for a date. Later, Kildare and Phelan go to Evy's apartment where they see her ending a date.

Evy later takes an overdose of sleeping pills and Phelan, who loves her, asks Kildare to leave her alone. Kildare, however, helps the couple reconcile with Gillespie saying he thinks that Evy needs therapy.

Writer: Jerry McNeely.

Director: Ralph Senensky.

Also appearing in this episode is Warren Kemmerling.

38. "Guest Appearance" October 25, 1962

Terry Galahad and a stage hand are injured on the set of his father's TV talk show. When Terry dies, Ted Galahad (Jack Carter) confronts Kildare, who was on the ambulance crew that came to the scene, about what happened.

Dr. Harold Ramey, Galahad's own doctor, tells Gillespie that Kildare did all that he could. Kildare watches a tape of the TV show to review his actions although Gillespie advises him not to pursue the matter.

Kildare says he won't accept a transfer to another hospital and says he's going on the Galahad show to discuss the incident. Gillespie also comes on the show with a tape showing what actually happened. Galahad apologizes to the doctors.

Writer: Archie L. Tegland.

Director: William Graham.

Other guests: Georgeann Johnson, Bert Remsen and S. John Launer. Launer often played a judge on *Perry Mason*.

39. "Hastings' Farewell" November 1, 1962

Gerald Hastings (Harry Guardino) is suffering from aphasia as the result of an automobile accident. His wife (Beverly Garland) is planning to put him in a nursing home. Kapish and Kildare discuss the case.

Kildare passes on a double date with Kapish so he can visit the aphasia unit at a VA hospital. In a visit to the Hastings home, Kildare sees home movies showing Hastings' condition before the accident. Mrs. Hastings says the couple's children are now living with their grandmother.

Writers: Peggy and Lou Shaw.

Director: Ralph Senensky.

Trivia: Kapish reports it rained during his date with the twins. Hastings kisses his wife on the forehead as a sign of farewell.

(Thanks to the Classic TV Archives for help on the following two episodes of Kildare which I have not been able to personally examine.)

*40. "Breakdown" November 8, 1962

Dr. Steven Waller (Larry Parks) believes that Kildare is out to destroy him.

Writer: Betty Andrews.

Director: Lawrence Dobkin.

Also appearing are Inga Swenson, Ellen Corby, Leslie Barrington, Norman Alden and Monte Burkhart.

*41. "The Cobweb Chain" November 15, 1962

A reprimand from Gillespie causes Dr. Chandra Ramid (Steven Hill) to near his breaking point. Also appearing in this episode are Clara Ray, Naomi Stevens and Joey Faye.

Writer: Ernest Kinoy

Director: Boris Sagal.

42. "The Soul Killer" November 22, 1962

Nurse Jenny Freesmith (Eileen Heckart) talks with Gillespie about her drug and alcohol problems. She then confronts Cathy Benjamin (Suzanne Pleshette) and a new nurse on her service.

Benjamin proposes a toast during a housewarming party at the home of Dr. and Mrs. John Grant (Bill Bixby, Barbara Parkins), then tells Kildare that she doesn't want to get serious. After morphine is stolen at Blair, Freesmith confronts Benjamin and finds the morphine.

Freesmith offers to help Benjamin and they go to a cabin Jenny owns. Meanwhile, Kildare and Gillespie search Freesmith's room and find her unused drug kit. On their way back to Blair, the nurses are injured in an accident. Freesmith keeps Benjamin from using morphine on her by breaking the bottle. Benjamin admits to the morphine theft and asks Gillespie for help.

Writer: George Eckstein.

Director: Elliot Silverstein.

43. "An Ancient Office" December 6, 1962

Kildare clashes with county coroner Henry Harris (Ed Begley) during a visit to his parents. He questions whether the death of an infant was a crib death as Harris has ruled and suggests an autopsy be conducted to determine the actual cause of death.

Gillespie, Kildare and his parents (Henderson Forsythe, Peggy Wood) discuss the lay coroner system. After an argument, Harris orders Kildare out of his house.

He then gets Gordon Hall, the child's father, a fulltime teaching job in the school system. Harris is also a member of the school board.

When Ellen Hall tries to commit suicide because she believes she killed her baby, Gordon authorizes the autopsy and Harris confronts him about that decision. Harris admits his error when the autopsy reveals that the baby died of a lung infection.

Writer: Theodore Apstein.

Director: Don Medford.

Dick Davalos is also featured in this episode.

Games people play: Gillespie and the senior Dr. Kildare play three games of chess with Gillespie winning all three. The Kildares then play a game.

44. "The Legacy" December 13, 1962

During Kildare's rotation on burn service, his newest patient is Luis Nieves (Mario Alcalde), who despite his burns can feel nothing. Kildare, chairman of the interns' activity committee, has a meeting with Miss Kyle, who's in charge of the nurses' activity committee.

When Kildare again examines Nieves, his wife (Olympia Dukakis) is confronting Jameson Black (Charles Macaulay), the other driver in the accident that caused her husband's injuries. Kildare tells Nieves that the burns destroyed his nerve endings and that is why he is feeling no pain.

Gillespie recalls his intern days when he and Kildare examine the new residence hall for Blair's interns. Kildare is worried about Nieves, who admits that he took a large dose of amphetamines before the accident.

Just before his death, Nieves sees his wife and son Pablo. Pablo plays while Mrs. Nieves and Kildare discuss whether or not she should sue Black. When she decides to sue, John Forsman (Edward Asner), the attorney for Black's insurance company asks to see Nieves' medical records.

During the trial, Mrs. Nieves testifies about her son's hopes for Pablo and it is proven that Nieves had the right-of-way. Kildare testifies about Nieves' health before the accident and that he had taken the dose of amphetamines. Mrs. Nieves is awarded $1,250 instead of the $10,000 she had sought.

Writer: John Furia Jr.

Director: Lamont Johnson.

Also appearing in this episode were Frank Killmond, Henry Beckman, Jo Helton, Bern Bassey, Rudy Corrella and Linda Bennett.

45. "The Bed I've Made" December 20, 1962

Veronica Johnson (Claire Trevor) is Blair's new director of nursing. After an argument with Gillespie, she talks with Jones, Blair's chief of public relations, about the difference between doctors and nurses. When Johnson and Gillespie go out to dinner, they discuss their work in London during World War II.

Gillespie is later admitted to Blair with a cold and Miss Phipps sends for Kildare. A student nurse, Miss Carroll (Jackie Joseph), "wins" the honor of giving Gillespie a sponge bath and she considers giving up nursing.

When Gillespie's fever shoots up to 105 degrees, Kildare has him put in an oxygen tent. Kildare and Johnson stay at Gillespie's bedside until he gets better. Gillespie refuses Johnson's resignation and tells her that she'll live up to her contract.

Writer: Jean Holloway.

Director: Don Taylor.

Other guests: Harriet MacGibbon, Robert Warwick, Hayden Rorke and Grandon Rhodes.

Berry-Pickings: Although he and Jackie Joseph were married at the time, Ken Berry says they never worked together on *Kildare*.

46. "A Time for Every Purpose" December 22, 1962

Kildare's newest patient is Millie Harper (Judee Morton), a teenager injured in an automobile accident. Mrs. Harper (Betty Field) authorizes an operation on her daughter but insists she not be told of the details on what has to be done.

The operation fails to save Millie's injured left eye and Mrs. Harper says she will choose the time to tell Millie what happened. Dr. Mattern (Murray Hamilton), the surgeon who operated on Millie, describes his program of treatment to Kildare, who then goes to the Harper home.

Kildare and Mrs. Harper tell Millie about her condition Mrs. Harper accepts a date for Millie while Gillespie criticizes Mattern for his treatment of the girl.

Kildare confronts Mrs. Harper about her actions while Gillespie talks with Millie. After Mrs. Harper sees how a nurse handles two blind children, she takes off Millie's eye patch and tells her daughter that she is beautiful.

Writers: Athur Weiss and Archie L. Tegland.

Director: Don Taylor.

Richard Eyer, Sheila Bromley, Sherry O'Neil and Nancy Lee also appeared in this episode.

47. "Love Is a Sad Song" January 3, 1963

Gillespie recommends Dr. Lilith MacGraw (Diana Hyland), who wants to be Blair's first woman surgeon, as the subject for a magazine article. Kildare and Agurski watch MacGraw's photo shoot while Jones interviews her.

MacGraw and Kildare later dine at the Starlight Room and then discuss their pasts on the way home. Later in the cafeteria, Kildare chooses MacGraw as a lunch companion instead of Agurski and Atkinson. Jones is later confronted by Drs. Lamb and Gillespie about the magazine article.

Gillespie asks Kildare about his interest in MacGraw. He then talks with the interns about their residency tests which Kildare, Agurski and MacGraw pass.

Writer: Jean Holloway.

Director: Boris Sagal.

Also appearing in this episode were Paul Langton, Oliver McGowan, Sidney May, Majel Barrett, Hugh Lawrence, Mary Webster, Alberta Nelson and Deidre.

Song: "Hi-Lili, Hi-Lo" (Chamberlain, with reprise by Hyland.)

48. "The Thing Speaks for Itself" January 10, 1963

Fashion designer Maxine Claudier dies while Kildare is running a test on her. Claudier's husband blames Blair for his wife's death and the hospital attorney

Arthur Hobler (Fritz Weaver) tells the doctors about his efforts on their behalf.

Dr. George Hazard (John Williams), who was once sued for malpractice, talks with Kildare about the situation. Kildare then talks with Rose Kemmer (Zohra Lampert), who is suffering from a heart condition, and who wants to see Hazard.

Hazard says Kemmer wouldn't survive her pregnancy. Kildare and Hazard argue about their differing positions on law and medicine.

After their appearance in court, Hobler questions Kildare and Gillespie about their treatment of Kemmer. Gillespie defends Kildare's skills as a doctor when questioned by Claudier's attorney Harper Faring. The suit is dismissed after Gillespie's testimony.

Writer: John W. Bloch.

Director: Don Medford.

Other guests in this episode were Jo Helton, Kelly Thordsen, Michelle Montau, Paul Newlan, Francis De Sales, Neil Rosso and Jess Kirkpatrick.

49. "The Great Guy" January 17, 1963

When comic Willie Guy (Jack Carter) is admitted to Blair, Kapish suggests that he could help Kildare with the annual hospital show. Kildare discusses Guy's condition with his wife (Constance Ford) and Gillespie says a biopsy is needed to determine is Guy's right leg tumor is benign or malignant.

Guy confronts the doctor after his right leg is amputated. Mrs. Guy forbids him to have any visitors while his colleague Ginger Sells (Jane Dulo) wonders what is going to happen with the hospital show.

Agurski tells Kildare that the show is in trouble. Sells sneaks into Guy's room where he calls her a stooge, then orders her to leave. Kildare and Mrs. Fain watch as Guy uses his crutches for the first time. Sells offers to help Kildare with the show during which she and Guy reconcile.

Writer/Director: James Komack.

The songs "We Are the Nurses" and "That's Entertainment" are part of this episode.

50. "The Mosaic" January 31, 1963

Tests reveal that medical student Charley Johnson (James Caan) is suffering from hepatitis. His fiancée Peggy Farrow (Barbara Barrie), also a medical student, wants to know what kind it is—serum or infectious. Kildare and Dr. William Ellis (Tom Tyron), who works for the health department, interview the other students in Johnson's class.

Two more cases are reported with one of the victims, Vernon, dying. Ellis gets a CDC report on hepatitis from his adoptive father while Gillespie finds out all the victims may have attended the same Christmas party. Johnson gets sicker as two more cases are reported. The doctors then discover that the hepatitis may have started in the medical school's hematology lab.

Writer: Jerry McNeely.

Director: David Lowell Rich.

Ben Wright also appeared in this episode.

*51. "Good Luck Charm" February 7, 1963

Actress Julia Colton (Gloria Swanson) suffers from a mysterious paralysis. Also appearing in this episode are Jena Engstrom and Jeanette Nolan.

Writers: Harry Kronman and James Komack.

Director: Jack Arnold.

*52. "Jail Ward" February 14, 1963

Kildare and Officer Stan Fisher (James Franciscus) clash over Fisher's efforts to get custody of a seriously ill man, who allegedly killed a fellow officer. Also featured in this episode, written by Jerome B. Thomas and directed by Jack Arnold, were Henry Silva, Ross Elliott, William Zuckert and Robert Strauss.

53. "A Trip to Niagara" February 21, 1963

Dr. Victor Jonah (John Larch) is inadvertently exposed to a dose of radiation while supervising a procedure. After the accident, Sara Anderson comes to see Jonah and tells him that she thinks she is suffering from Parkinson's disease.

The Jonahs discuss the Anderson case and their personal lives. Dr. Jonah later tells his wife that he is postponing their trip to Niagara Falls.

Jonah tries to comfort Anderson after she suffers an attack. He and Kildare then discuss the Anderson case with Kildare explaining the procedure, which will be done under a local anesthetic, to Anderson.

Writer: Gerald Sanford.

Director: Robert Gist.

Irene Dailey was also featured in this episode.

*54. "A Place Among the Monuments" February 28, 1963

Kildare stops a girl from committing suicide, but tragedy ensues in this episode written by Alvin Boretz and directed by William Graham. Guest stars were Harold J. Stone, Brendan Dillon, Aki Aleong, Sharon Conners and H. M. Wynant.

55. "Face of Fear" March 7, 1963

Matt Hendricks (Robert Culp) destroys a Blair laboratory, but nobody—not even Matt—knows that he is responsible. Kildare and Gillespie discuss Hendricks after Kildare treats him for a cut hand.

Hendricks goes to see his Aunt Frances (Mary Astor) and asks questions about what happened to his late father. They also discuss his mother's funeral and Aunt Frances says she'll take care of Matt.

Ellen Hendricks (Mariette Hartley) asks not to be excluded from her husband's life shortly before he assaults her and Kildare. Hendricks goes to his aunt's home where she gives him the room that was his father's.

When Ellen and Kildare come to her home, Frances admits that Matt's father unknowingly killed his wife. Matt's going to a waterfront bar for a drink leads to him fighting with two policemen. Tests show that Matt, who is suffering from a form of epilepsy, can be helped with medication.

Writer: Betty Andrews.

Director: David Friedkin.

Dan Frazer also appeared in this episode.

56. "Sister Mike" March 14, 1962

Gillespie talks with Kildare about a community center where he's working. It's run by Sister Mike (Fay Bainter), who confronts Lorena Henty (Collin Wilcox) about how she treats her children.

Sister Mike later sends Kildare to a bar for the PA system it is loaning to the center for a program. Gillespie helps Sister Mike with the program. Jody and Cora Sue, Lorena's children, listen while Cora Sue is fixing dinner. Jody is later badly burned in a fire and is treated by Gillespie and Kildare. Kildare finds Lorena at the bar and Lorena asks Sister Mike to see Jody with her.

Writers: John T. Dugan and John W. Bloch.

Director: Elliot Silverstein.

Trivia: Mary Badham, who plays Cora Sue in this episode, is probably best known for playing Scout in *To Kill a Mockingbird*.

57. "A Very Infectious Disease" March 21, 1963

Kildare is in charge of the infectious disease unit where Dr. Phillip Downey (Daniel O'Herlihy) is also assigned. Munoz (Vito Scotti), a patient Downey has been abusing, tries to escape. Meanwhile, Downey forms a rapport with a young patient named Jerry Tucker.

Kildare and Gillespie both confront Downey about his actions. Nurse Mary Ogilvy (Jean Hagen) watches Downey as he interacts with Tucker.

Downey admits to his feelings of prejudice, which he says come from an incident in his native Australia. Downey and Ogilvy discuss their pasts with Downey admitting he's not sure where he'll practice after completing his residency.

Downey resigns just before Gillespie would have dismissed him. Gillespie says that Munoz won't be deported and Munoz apologizes for his behavior in the unit.

Writers: Robert and Wanda Duncan.

Director: Jules Bricken.

*58. "Dark Side of the Mirror" March 28, 1963

Polly Bergen plays a dual role in the story of a woman who refuses to donate a kidney to her twin sister. Also featured in the episode are Alex Nicol, Ron Sumner, Peggy Ream, Jason Johnson, Jennifer Gillespie and Harold Gould. The episode was written by William Bast and Dick Nelson and directed by Lamont Johnson.

59. "The Sleeping Princess" April 11, 1963

Kildare finds Sophia Niachos (June Harding) in her apartment when he goes on an ambulance call. Her father Nick (Charles H. Radilac) is suffering from a terminal brain tumor. Kildare asks Nick why he kept his daughter isolated from the world.

After Sophia undergoes a series of tests, Dr. Meadows, a hospital psychiatrist, says she's not suffering from any mental problems but Kildare disagrees and says Sophia shouldn't be released. Gillespie finds a couple to be foster parents for Sophia but she doesn't like the idea. Mrs. Trumbull, who used to be a private duty nurse for Gillespie, and Kildare watch as Sophia begins to isolate herself.

Sophia goes to her father's hospital room just after his death. Meadows believes that a week in the Trumbull home would help Sophia more than a month of therapy would. Gillespie believes that Sophia has become too attached to both the hospital and Kildare. Kildare says Sophia shouldn't retreat to her fantasy world anymore.

Writer: Archie L. Tegland.

Director: Lamont Johnson.

Also featured in this episode were Martine Bartlett, Moyna MacGill, Romney Tree, Carol Stone and Alex Davion.

60. "Ship's Doctor" April 18, 1963

Gillespie wins a three-day cruise in a raffle from a ticket Kildare sold him. He asks cruise director Sharon Calloway (Elinor Donahue) and fellow passenger D. V. Dromly (John Fiedler), a regular Blair patient, to keep his profession a secret from everyone including ship's doctor Harvey Jones (Patrick O'Neal).

Mrs. Kovar (Magda Harvat), a pregnant passenger, talks with Jones about her condition. The Kovars are on their second honeymoon. Gillespie is told by the ship's captain how much Jones has improved the ship's medical facilities.

Jones discovers that Dromly is not a doctor as he had thought. Gillespie tells Jones that he is a doctor just before they examine Dromly, who has accidentally poisoned himself. The doctors also work together to deliver the Kovars' baby.

Calloway tells Jones that she is the company inspector, and not Gillespie, as Jones had suspected.

Writers: Arthur Ross and Archie L. Tegland.

Director: Jack Arnold.

Also featured: Dub Taylor, Robert Casper, Claudine Longet, Cynthia Lynn, Orville Sherman, Ron Whelan, Anthony Eastrel and Stefan Gierasch.

*61. "Tightrope Into Nowhere" April 25, 1963

Peggy Shaw wrote this episode in which Kildare questions the treatment of a terminally ill patient. Elliot Silverstein directed the show which featured Mary Murphy, Edward Asner and Josie Lloyd as guests.

62. "The Balance and the Crucible" May 2, 1963

When Dr. Matt Gunderson (Peter Falk) is offered a residency at Blair after his wife Emily leaves for a mission in South America, he asks Kildare for advice. Gunderson, who is also a minister, suffers a crisis of faith after Emily (Sue Randall) is killed.

Kildare and Gunderson later argue about the existence of God, whom Gunderson no longer believes in. They also disagree about Gunderson's refusal to serve as a minister when the hospital's Protestant chaplain, Dr. Ashburn, is not available. When the patient Gunderson refuses to help dies, Gunderson goes to the hospital roof and breaks down, calling Emily and God's names, and asking God for help.

Writer: Jerry McNeely.

Director: Don Medford.

Bill Bixby, June Vincent, Noreen Corcoran and Anne Loos are also featured in this episode. Sue Randall, who portrayed Emily, is best known as Miss Landers on *Leave It to Beaver.*

63. "The Gift of the Koodjanuk" May 9, 1963

Kildare's newest patient is his uncle Alfred Freely (Brian Keith), who claims the koodjanuk he hangs on his bed is a good luck charm. Kildare and Gillespie discuss why he put Freely on Ward B, a unit where a number of patients have recently died.

The Ward B patients "adopt" astronaut William Singer, who Freely says is also his nephew. Freely tells Kildare that he fears the operation that he needs. Claire Gebhardt, Freely's niece by marriage, comes to see him and talk about why he left the Gebhardt home with Freely admitting that he is a con man.

Freely tries to aid Tonio Pronesti (Al Ruscio) while the other Ward B patients listen. Freely says goodbye to his fellow patients as he has found that his tumor is inoperable and that he only has a few days to live.

Writer: Walter Brough.

Director: William Graham.

Also featured in this episode are Greg Morris, Joseph Perry, J. Pat O'Malley, Joseph Sweeney and Jean Allison.

64. "An Island Like A Peacock" May 16, 1963

Gina Beemis (Kathryn Hays) and her father Max (Forrest Tucker), who abandoned the blind woman when she was a child, argue with her friend Harry (Leonard Nimoy) serving as a witness. The argument leads to Max being hospitalized.

Kildare tells Gina that an operation could restore her eyesight. Beemis gives Kildare a $5,000 check to give to Gina. When Kildare and Gina argue over the check, Kildare asks Gina if she's ever gone to the Braille Institute. (The Institute provided technical assistance for the episode.)

Beemis decides to will his eyes to Gina and gets away from Blair, meeting Gina and Harry outside their workplace. Gina and her father talk about fantasies and Beemis leaves Gina to find her way around the pier.

Writer: Gerald Sanford.

Director: Elliot Silverstein.

Also featured in this episode were Lillian Bronson, Eli Mintz, Marjorie Bennett, Curt Barrett, Marcia Blakesley and Carol Andreson.

65. "To Each His Own Prison" May 23, 1963

Kildare's newest patient, Oscar Clayton (Ross Martin) is suffering from delirium tremens. Gillespie discusses Clayton's condition with his wife. Before he lapses into a coma, Clayton confesses to an embezzlement for which his partner was convicted.

Judge Manning, an old friend of Gillespie's, discusses Clayton's problem with the doctors. A hearing is held during which Kildare reports Clayton's crime. When Kildare confronts Clayton, his former patient confesses that he is drinking again. Clayton finds a bottle of whiskey after the bar he is drinking at closes, but he breaks the bottle, and gets the DTs again. Back at Blair, Clayton decides to let the doctors help him.

Writer: Betty Andrews.

Director: Don Medford.

Other guests in this episode are George Kennedy, Lois Smith, Anne Meecham, Regis Toomey, Edgar Buchanan, Jared Barclay, John Marley and Bobby Pickett.

Dr. Phyllis Wright took over as the show's technical advisor.

Gillespie compares alcoholics to lemmings. Gillespie, Manning and Kildare play a game of pool.

66. "A Hand Held Out in Darkness" May 30, 1963

Kildare does not know the name of his newest patient, a little girl he names Charlie Jane Doe. Sgt. Smith (Philip Abbott), the detective in charge of Charlie's case, calls to check on her condition. Meanwhile, Gillespie brings in a sick baby, his grandson Leonard. Dr. George Miller examines young Leonard and then temporarily bars Gillespie from the room while Nurse Fain tells Kildare that there have been a number of calls about the baby.

Dr. David Key, Blair's newest psychiatrist, examines Charlie and wonders why the little girl can't speak. When Charlie sees a doll, she runs to Kildare and Gillespie thinks the doll sparked a memory in Charlie. Kildare later takes Charlie on a walk through the neighborhood where she was found and then one through a nearby neighborhood. When her memories come back, Charlie runs off and leads Kildare to where someone killed her Aunt Kate. Gillespie is allowed to take his grandson.

Writer: Jean Holloway.

Director: Robert Gist.

Also featured in this episode were Wilton Graff, Vicki Cos, Paul Mantee, Anita Dangler, Richard Benjamin, Valora Noland, Joey Scott, Dorothy Neumann and Gilbert Green.

67. "What's God to Julius?" June 6, 1963

Kildare examines Benny Orloff (Martin Balsam) in Blair's outpatient ward while his mentally challenged brother Julius (Sorrell Booke) waits in the lobby. Orloff tells Kildare about his brother and the brothers discuss about the hospital Julius used to live in.

Benny is suffering from liver cancer and Gillespie asks what will happen to Julius after Benny is gone. Kildare finds a job for Julius in the hospital cafeteria. When Julius and Benny have an argument, Julius runs away from the hospital.

Writer: Adrian Spies.

Director: Robert Gist.

Also featured in this episode were Wallace Rooney, John Bliefer, Jack Bernardi, Maura McGiveney and Max Hoffman.

§

Raymond Massey.

Chapter 4

The Third
TV Season

September 26, 1963
to May 21, 1964

T he third season began on September 26, 1963 with Steven Bell as Dr. Quint Lowry, Jo Helton as Nurse Conant and Barbara Bell Wright as Nurse Currier joining the cast.

68. "Whoever Heard of a Two-Headed Doll?" September 26, 1963

Kildare, who's about to become a resident, is treating real estate developer Harry Gregg (Charles Bronson) for leukemia. Gregg's wife Lila (Janice Rule) was a friend of Kildare's in high school.

Gillespie and Kildare discuss how to tell the Greggs about Harry's condition and Lila asks Kildare why Harry was moved to a private room. After learning Harry has invested all the family's money, Kildare tells Lila about Harry's condition and this provokes an argument between him and Lila.

Writer: Jerry McNeely.

Director: Don Medford.

David Whorf, Charity Grace and Richard Anderson were also featured in this episode.

69. "The Good Samaritan" October 3, 1963

Kildare delivers a baby 30 miles from the nearest hospital with the grandmother's help. The mother survives but the baby doesn't and Kildare is sued for malpractice by the Cullen family.

Fred Payson (Leonard Stone), the insurance company's attorney, recommends that Kildare settle but he refuses. During the trial, Gillespie and Bromley (Thomas Gomez) have a confrontation in the courthouse hallway. The Cullen family gets a $55,000 judgment against Kildare.

Writer: Donald S. Sanford.

Director: Elliot Silverstein.

Also featured in this episode were John Anderson, Ruth White, Jennifer Billingsley, Paul Barselow, Rhys Williams and Steve Gravers.

Trivia: The Hospital of the Good Samaritan, Los Angeles, CA, provided technical assistance through the history of the show.

70. "If You Can't Believe the Truth" October 10, 1963

Judy Gail (Barbara Eden), the sister of Kildare's college roommate, comes to visit Blair and gets a job as a nurse. The first people Kildare introduces her to are Kapish and Paul Garrett (Bob Denver), two of his fellow interns. Kapish appoints himself as a committee of one to show Judy around Blair.

Tycoon Henry Kincaid (James Whitmore), Kildare's newest patient, is suffering from an ulcer. While Kincaid is being examined, Judy who wants to find a rich man to marry, checks his financial status.

Kincaid authorizes surgery but says he has some affairs to arrange first. Kildare suddenly develops a sneezing problem that Garrett traces to Judy's perfume.

Writer: Irene Winston.

Director: John Newland.

Also featured in this episode were James Hampton, Mary Webster, Joan Young, Paullie Clark, Elizabeth Fraser, Arthur Hanson and William Lanteau.

Berry -Pickings: This was the first time future *F-Troop*ers Hampton and Berry worked together and they've been friends ever since. Berry recalls director Newland saying that his character (Kapish) should get the girl for once. His kiss with Eden was his first screen kiss. The scene was a rare improvisation in a *Kildare* episode.

71. "The Heart, an Imperfect Machine" October 17, 1963

Emma Swoder (Diane Baker), the wife of the inventor of a heart/lung machine who Kildare is working with, requests immediate surgery on her heart when Gillespie examines her. Swoder (Pat Hingle) tries to convince Emma to postpone the surgery so he can improve the machine.

Kildare offers to aid Swoder, who angrily turns him down. Emma later talks about her life with Kildare. Gillespie orders Kildare to operate the heart/lung machine during Emma's surgery that Dr. Haskert is in charge of.

Writers: Pete Morrow and Dick Nelson.

Director: Robert Butler.

Susan Brown and Carol Andreson were also featured in this episode.

72. "A Game for Three" October 24, 1963

Dr Louis Miller (Andrew Prine) asks Kildare why he doesn't like him Kildare is later a guest for dinner at the Miller home where Miller asks Kildare to be his wife Barbara's (Susan Strasberg) doctor.

When Miller improperly administers a drug to a patient, Gillespie thinks the incident should go on his record. Meanwhile, Miller thinks Kildare is falling in love with Barbara, who is suffering from a kidney ailment.

Miller later claims that Kildare has been pursuing his wife, but Gillespie doesn't believe him. Barbara tells Kildare that she is going to have a baby. At Miller's hearing, Gillespie calls both Millers as witnesses and Barbara exposes her husband as a liar. Miller is suspended from duty.

Writer: Jerry McNeely.

Director: Paul Wendkos.

Also appearing in this episode were Les Tremayne, Adrienne Marden and Charles Lampkin.

73. "The Exploiters" October 31, 1963

Wally, an orderly at Blair, is furnishing Brown's Funeral Home with the names of recently deceased patients. Meanwhile, Kildare has a confrontation with Jean Dennis (Nancy Malone), a special nurse, whose father is dying. Kildare later apologizes to Dennis and promises to keep an eye on her father.

After Dennis dies, Brown (Judson Laire) comes to see the family and discovers that Dennis wanted a large funeral. Kildare keeps a salesman from cheating Mrs. Dennis.

Gillespie and Brown argue about the ethics of the funeral home business when Brown complains about Kildare's actions. When Jean doesn't go to her father's funeral, Tommy Dennis asks for Kildare's help in finding his sister and also tells Brown off. Jean later reconciles with her mother.

Writers: Richard Levinson and William Link.

Director: Leonard Horn.

Crahan Denton, Tommy Farrell, Johnny Washbrook, Arthur Peterson, Cathy Birch and Vic Tayback also appeared in this episode.

74. "One Clear, Bright Thursday Morning" November 7, 1963

Hana Shigera (Miyoshi Umeki) tells Kildare that she lived in Negasaki when it was bombed during World War II when she comes to him for a pregnancy checkup. She later tells her husband Roy (James Shigeta), who is on staff at Blair, about it when he comes home from work.

Dr. Lenlow, a hematologist, takes blood samples from Hana that are studied by Gillespie and Kildare. They tell Roy that Hana might have leukemia but that more tests are required. Kildare tells Hana that they'll do all they can for her baby and Hana gives him a geisha doll named Lotus Blossom.

Hana and her mother-in-law argue about where the baby will be raised just before Hana has a fainting spell. At the hospital, Hana asks Kildare to save the baby and look after Roy. When Hana survives, Roy goes to the hospital chapel to pray.

Writers: Margaret and Paul Schneider.

Director: Leonard Horn.

Parley Baer and Garry Walberg, who would later be a regular on *Quincy, M.E.,* were also featured in this episode.

75. "The Eleventh Commandment" November 14, 1963

Ida Forman (Molly Picon) and Carol Logan (Susan Oliver), Kildare's newest patients, share a room at Blair. Gillespie tells Logan that she is suffering from myasthenia gravis, which can be regulated with medication.

Logan faints after an argument with Forman, who later introduces Logan to her son Julian (Michael Forrest), an art professor. Gillespie talks with Forman's children about her health while Logan tells Gillespie that she's going to be a freelance artist.

Gillespie and Forman discuss King Lear with Gillespie quoting from the play as they discuss her past and future.

Writers: Theodore Apstein and Sidney A. Mandel.

Director: John Newland.

Lurene Tuttle also appeared in this episode.

Trivia: According to Ken Berry, Chamberlain often used a skateboard to get around the *Kildare* set.

76. "Four Feet in the Morning" November 21, 1963

This was the first of a two-part crossover story which concluded on *The Eleventh Hour* on November 27, 1963. Show stars Ralph Bellamy and Jack Ging were among the guests on this episode.

Kildare and Gillespie examine Darlene Landon (Marta Kristen), whose parents are old friends of Gillespie's. Kildare tells Darlene that she is three months pregnant and Gillespie talks with her about her condition.

Bob Quincy (Tony Dow), Darlene's boyfriend and the baby's father, talks with his mother (Ruth Roman) about the situation and she tells him about her past. Bob and Dr. L. Richard Starke (Bellamy) discuss the situation while Mrs. Quincy talks with Gillespie and Kildare.

Bob goes to see Darlene while Gillespie, Kildare and Dr. Paul Graham (Ging) meet with the Landons. Mrs. Landon tells Bob that the baby is being put up for adoption while Starke and Gillespie discuss Bob's case. They also discuss the Riddle of the Sphinx.

Writer: Jerry De Bono.

Director: Jack Smight.

Andrew Duggan and Richard Carlyle also appeared in this episode, which featured Chris Crosby's song "Young and In Love."

Tony Dow and Ralph Bellamy in a two-part crossover story with *The Eleventh Hour* titled "Four Feet in the Morning."

77. "The Pack Rat and the Prima Donna" November 28, 1963

Kildare's new assignment is working with Nurse Jane Munson (Celeste Holm) in Blair's Central Supply. Munson, the department supervisor, has repeated run-ins with Dr. Keith Judge (Ed Nelson), who works in Blair's burn unit. One of them concerns his placing an order using data from an 1893 catalog.

Nurse Danielle Mercier (Danielle de Metz), a native of France, talks with Kildare about how medicine is practiced in France before they make plans for a date.

Writer: James Gunn.

Director: Paul Wendkos.

*78. "The Backslider" December 5, 1963

Gillespie investigates a staff doctor, whose carelessness endangers patients. Guests in this episode were Kevin McCarthy, Anne Helm, Josie Lloyd and Harry Ellerbe.

Writer: Archie L. Tegland.

Director: John Newland.

79. "Charlie Wade Makes Lots of Shade" December 12, 1963

Kildare and Wade (Dale Malone) discuss his physical condition, which is affecting Wade's vision. John and Sarah Oliver, his brother-in-law and sister (Frank Overton, Mary LaRoche), discuss Wade's going out on his own after Charlie gets angry with their daughter Sandy.

Kildare discuss obesity and compulsive overeating as well as the Wade case. Wade is now a diabetic and gets hospitalized as a result. While there, he reads the story of Goldilocks and the Three Bears to the patients in the pediatrics unit. The Olivers and Kildare search for Wade when he leaves the hospital and they find him at the diner where he had gone blind earlier.

Writers: Jerry McNeely and Dr. Marshall Goldberg.

Director: Allen Miner.

Marion Ross (later of *Happy Days*), Jonathan Kidd, Claire Wilcox, Carol Seflinger and Anna Capri were also featured in this episode.

80. "The Oracle" December 19, 1963

Virginia Herson (Lauren Bacall), a newspaper columnist and an old friend of Gillespie's, is one of Kildare's new patients. She and Suzie Walker (Brenda Scott) are both suffering from multiple sclerosis. During grand rounds, Suzie answers questions about her condition from Kildare's students.

Gillespie gives a lecture on the disease's history while Herson tries to commit suicide with a bottle of sleeping pills supplied by her secretary, Ruth Scully (Joyce Van Patten). Gillespie tells Herson what he thinks of her actions while Suzie's baby is delivered while Kildare watches.

Writer: Gene Wang.

Director: Jack Smight.

Also featured in this episode were Adam Williams, Staats Cotsworth, William Sargent, Jocelyn Brando, Charles Krung and Vida Harris.

81. "A Vote of Confidence" December 26, 1963

Dr. Norman French (Eddie Albert) is hosting a party at which Gillespie is a guest. French is considering a run against Gillespie for the chief of staff post at Blair.

Gillespie tells Dr. George Garrison (Carl Benton Reid) that he is considering retirement. Meanwhile, Agurski begins a pool on who'll be elected chief of staff and Kildare bets on Gillespie.

French hears his associate, Dr. Jerry Helvick (Frank Aletter) tells Gillespie about his affair with Dr. Susan Merrivale. Kildare borrows cuff links from Agurski and then discusses the chief of staff election with Gillespie over a game of chess. Gillespie decides he still wants the job and wins the election over French.

Writers: Richard Levinson and William Link.

Director: Paul Wendkos.

Gene Blakely, Lizabeth Hush and Patricia Breslin also appeared in this episode.

82. "A Willing Suspension of Disbelief" January 9, 1964

Kildare wakes Dr. Frank Michaels (Jack Lord) from a nightmare caused by a drug overdose. Michaels tells Gillespie about the situation and talks with Kildare about his marriage. Monte, a trainer, tells Michaels that he has arthritis and recommends that Michaels sample a new drug that could help cure arthritis.

Michaels wants his wife not to tell Kildare or Gillespie what's wrong with him. R. E. Lenger (Denver Pyle) tells Michaels about lachimal, the drug which he claims cured him in two months. After a confrontation with Kildare, Michaels talks about the standards at Blair.

Gillespie tells Michaels and Lowry about an operation Michaels is scheduled to perform. After Michaels slugs Kildare, then runs from the hospital, Gillespie thinks Michaels is suffering from manic depression. Kildare and Michaels later discuss a program of treatment.

Writer: Harold Gast

Director: Leonard Horn.

Also featured in this episode were Mala Powers, Patience Cleveland and Della Sharman.

83 and 84. "Tyger, Tyger" January 16 and 23, 1964

Kildare examines Pat Holmes (Yvette Mimieux) after she falls off her surf board three times. After he fails to get a medical history, Kildare talks with her parents and later must tell Pat that she must give up surfing.

Dr. Norman Gage (Clu Gulager) comes to visit Pat in the hospital, then talks with Kildare about Pat and his own medical background. Paul Montgomery (John Newland, who directed many Kildare episodes, including doing double-duty acting in and directing this one), a Blair board member and friend of Gillespie's, is worried about his wife, Carol (Anjanette Comer), who is an alcoholic.

Kildare and Gillespie discuss the similarities between Pat and Carol. Gage calls Kildare and says Pat is surfing again. While Gillespie and Kildare examine Pat, Carol leaves the hospital and Kildare finds her at a bar. The two women become roommates at Blair.

Pat helps Kildare shop for a surf board and then takes him out for a lesson. Another seizure sends Pat back to the hospital while Montgomery tells his wife that she wants a divorce.

Pat and Carol go to the beach where Gage helps them search for sea life. Carol fails to talk Pat out of surfing and she is struck by a fatal seizure.

Writer: Ben Mosselink.

George Petrie also appeared in this episode.

Song: "My Precious One" (Chamberlain)

85. "Never Too Old for the Circus" January 30, 1964

Dr. Charles Priest (Walter Pidgeon), an old friend of Gillespie's, wants to return to work. Kildare's father refers a case to Blair while Priest tells his wife that he is coming out of retirement.

Blair has a new diagnostic computer and one of its first cases involves Calhoun, the machine's designer. Kildare and Priest have an argument about Priest's conduct and Gillespie asks Kildare to apologize. When Priest's grandson Chris becomes ill, he refuses to let Priest examine him. Kildare offers his help and winds up going to the circus with Chris, Gillespie and Priest.

Writers: Jameson Brewer and Eric Peters.

Director: Paul Wendkos.

Ann Harding, John Fiedler, Joey Scott and Barry Atwater are also featured in this episode.

*86. "Onions, Garlic and the Flowers That Bloom in the Spring" February 6, 1964

Writer: Theodore Apstein.

Director: John Newland.

Featured in this episode are Cesar Romero, Audrey Dalton, Joe DeSantis, Marianna Hill, Nick Alexander and James Noah.

87. "To Walk in Grace" February 13, 1964

Gillespie assigns Kildare to help author Helen Scott (Gena Rowlands) research her next book. Kildare takes her on a tour around Blair, including a visit to the pediatrics ward.

Kildare later drives Scott home where they discuss her creation of a doctor who falls in love with an author. Gillespie gives Kildare a copy of Scott's latest novel, which she dedicated to Gillespie. Kildare is whom she dedicates her next book to.

Writer: Joy Dexter.

Director: Ida Lupino.

Also featured in this episode were Brenda Scott, James Griffith, Michel Petit and Joan Tompkins.

88. "Goodbye, Mr. Jersey" February 20, 1964

Ellen Adams (Suzanne Pleshette) tries to smuggle an English sheepdog named Mr. Jersey into the hospital with help from Kapish and Kildare. The dog was injured by a hit-and-run driver. Dr. Tex Mantell (Fred Beir) is drafted into helping with the dog.

Gillespie tells the hospital board that he will resign if either Kildare or Mantell are given trouble about caring for Mr. Jersey.

Kildare finds himself acting in a commercial for Schultz's Moravian Stout as a favor to Ellen, who is an actress. A benefit for Mr. Jersey is held at Mantell's house during which Mr. Jersey chooses a friend of Gillespie's as his new master.

Writer: Irene Winston.

Director: John Newland

John Banner, who later played Schultz on *Hogan's Heroes*, also played a character named Schultz in this episode. Also featured were J. Pat O'Malley, Peggy Rea, Max Showalter, Arthur Malet, Bert Remsen, Marion Collier, Anthony Holland and Chet Stratton.

89. "Why Won't Anyone Listen?" February 27, 1964

Edward Fredericks (Claude Rains) talks with two friends (William Demarest, Burt Mustin) about the death of his granddaughter Peggy after a tonsillectomy. One of them suggests that he go to see the head of the hospital.

Fredericks gets a book about building bombs and then calls Gillespie using a tape Peggy made before her death. He makes a bomb, hiding it in a first aid kit, which he then puts in a briefcase. He puts it in Gillespie's bookcase, and then reveals the bomb. Kildare, Lowry and Gillespie guide Fredericks out of the hospital and a police officer guides him to a park across the street from Blair. The bomb explodes before the bomb squad can take it from Fredericks.

Writer: Calvin Clements.

Director: John Newland.

Also appearing in this episode were Peter Hansen, Walter Brooke, Ted de Corsia, Susan Brown, Irene Martin, James Nolan and Robert Cole.

90. "The Child Between" March 5, 1964

Kildare discusses the case of diabetic Bobby Colby (Beau Bridges) with his divorced parents (Lee Phillips, Jeanne Cooper). Kildare then examines Bobby and counsels his mother Marion to get some rest.

Bobby doesn't eat breakfast the next morning and he tells Kildare that his condition makes him special. Linda Robbins, who is also a diabetic and who attends a camp Kildare operates, is one of Bobby's visitors.

Bobby goes to the camp after his mother rejects the idea of psychiatric care for him. When he goes two days without an insulin injection, he goes into a coma.

Writer: Philip Saltzman.

Director: Allen Miner.

Jan Moriarty, Allan Hunt and Brooke Bundy also appeared in this episode.

91. "A Hundred Million Tomorrows" March 12, 1964

Oil executive Lawrence Crane (Paul Burke), a member of Blair's board, is treated by Kildare and Gillespie. Crane has a heart attack and asks the doctor to contact his firm's executive vice president Don Martin (George Grizzard). Crane promotes Martin and sends him to a meeting in London.

Lionel Grant, one of the firm's largest stockholders, offers to buy the company and Martin asks for the offer to put in writing. Crane fires Martin briefly when he finds out about his actions, and then rehires him as a partner.

Writer: Jerome B. Thomas.

Director: Don Medford.

Also appearing in this episode were Diana van der Vlis, Robert Brubaker, David Whorf, Hilary Wontner, William Woodson and Dennis Patrick.

Medical note: Crane calls Gillespie "Dr. G," a nickname Lew Ayres used in *The Story of Dr. Kildare* radio series.

92. "Tomorrow Is A Fickle Girl" March 19, 1964

Carlos Mendoza (Sal Mineo), Kildare's newest patient, takes a Blair prescription pad because he is posing as a doctor in his neighborhood. Mendoza is suffering from a heart condition.

Kildare tracks Mendoza to the office of Dr. Valdes, and then confronts him about the stolen prescription blanks. Mendoza tells Kildare that Valdes has been dead for six weeks and Kildare offers to help Mendoza.

Mendoza's mother, who has been suffering from headaches, is brought to Blair where she dies despite the doctors' best efforts. Gillespie gets Mendoza a job in Blair's laboratory.

Writer: James F. Griffith.

Director: Paul Wendkos.

Also featured in this episode are Naomi Stevens, Leonid Kinskey, Manuel Padilla and Roberto Contreras.

93. "Quid Pro Quo" March 26, 1964

Kildare is supervising a group of interns that includes Neal Tomlinson and Chuck Deveraux (Robert Walker, Michael Callan). Gillespie shows Kildare and Lowry a patient who was bitten by a black widow spider after which Kildare has a confrontation with Devereaux about his future in medicine.

When Gillespie confronts Devereaux about making a treatment error, the intern confesses to being drunk. This results in his suspension and a meeting with the dean of the medical school. Tomlinson confesses to making the error Devereaux took the blame for and then commits suicide. Devereaux finds the body, and then has an argument with Kildare.

Writer: Archie L. Tegland.

Director: Don Medford.

Barry Maccollum, Anne Loos, Holly McIntire, Robert B. Williams, Kirk Elliott and Cheryl Holdridge also appeared in this episode.

94. "A Day to Remember" April 2, 1964

Kildare assigns Nora Willis (Anne Baxter) as a volunteer to care for hematology patient Jerry Schell (Michel Petit), unaware she was turned down because of a long volunteer waiting list. The hospital tries to contact his stepmother Carol Devon (Yvonne Craig) but she ducks the call.

Kildare later goes to the club where Devon works and talks with her about Jerry. Gillespie orders Jerry's transfer to pediatrics just before Nora and Jerry sneak out of the hospital. They go to an amusement park where Jerry passes while on a ride. Kildare and Gillespie tell Nora that Jerry will be fine.

Writer: Calvin Clements.

Director: John Newland.

Edith Atwater, Jon Lormer, Josie Lloyd, Ken Mayer, Natalie Core, Bill Bradley and Mary Lansing also appear in this episode.

Song: "I Fall in Love Too Easily" (Craig).

95. "An Ungodly Act" April 9, 1964

Kildare brings Ana Martinez to Blair when he fails to get her admitted to East Knolls Hospital, which is actually closer to her mother's home. Despite Kildare and Lowry's best efforts, Ana dies and Kildare has to tell her mother.

Gillespie confronts Dr. Robert Devlin (Douglas Fairbanks, Jr.), the East Knolls administrator, about the matter and Devlin demands a retraction of an interview Kildare gave about the situation with Hospital attorney Fred Payson (Leonard Stone). Meanwhile, Nurse Leah Bradley, who was with Kildare at the time of the incident, tears up the retraction.

Writer: Calvin Clements.

Director: Don Medford.

Also appearing in this episode were Susan Bay, Shelley Morrison, Mary Jackson, Herb Ellis, Paul Nowlan and Beverly Adams.

96. "A Nickel's Worth of Prayer" April 16, 1964

Joe Hogan (Ed Begley), who is suffering from cancer, needs more surgery but argues with Kildare about it. Hogan gets a birthday card from Patsy (Kim Darby), a little girl he befriended. While looking at the card, Hogan recalls his days as an apartment superintended.

Patsy and her mother (Lola Albright) argue about her skipping school just before she goes to see Hogan. Gillespie and Kildare find Joe, Patsy and Joe's roommates singing. Hogan advises Patsy to stay in school and help her mother.

Writer: Agnes Ridgway.

Director: John Newland.

Steve Mitchell, Beverly Adams, Linda Evans, Judy Carne and Roy Glenn were also featured in this episode.

97. "Night of the Beast" April 23, 1964

Dr. Lois Bower (Carol Rossen) helps Kildare and Kapish treat a patient before they go off duty. Gillespie and Kildare later examine Jeannie Sawyer (Sharon Farrell), a drug overdose victim, who refuses to take her medication.

Tony Warren (Bradford Dillman), an acquaintance of Sawyer), later asks Bower for a date but she turns him down. When Kildare and Bower leave a theater where they saw the silent version of Ben-Hur, Warren and his gang are waiting for them. They follow the doctors to the beach where they assault Bower.

Kildare goes looking for Warren while Kapish and Gillespie are treating patients who are suffering from methyl alcohol blindness.

When Kildare finds Warren at his latest hangout, the two fight, and Bower identifies Warren after his arrest.

Writer: Richard Fielder.

Director: James Goldstone.

Also appearing in this episode are Ivan Dixon, Kate Murtagh and Hal K. Dawson.

Dillman's take: In a letter to the author, Dillman reports that he helped train Chamberlain for their fight scene and helped choreograph it. Kildare's foes were usually diseases or other doctors. Dillman also made an observation that this author agrees with, based on his watching of *Kildare* episodes: Raymond Massey (Gillespie) was kept moving because when he sat down, the scene involved was usually drained of energy.

98. "The Middle of Ernie Mann" April 30, 1964

Kildare conducts a physical on old friend and boxer Ernie Mann (Terry Carter), but the results are inconclusive. After Kildare and Gillespie discuss boxing, they meet with Dr. Franklin (Peter Whitney) of the state Boxing Commission. Both Franklin and Gillespie boxed in their younger days.

Roy Winters (Tige Andrews), Mann's manager, is concerned about him. When Kildare visits Mann at the school where he's a volunteer, Mann's son Davey invites him to dinner.

The doctors discover Mann is suffering from an ulcer but he insists on fighting anyway. Kildare and his colleagues watch Mann's fight with champion Jackie Pollard on TV. Franklin brings Mann to Blair after the fight.

Writers: Margaret and Paul Schneider.

Director: Don Medford.

Also featured in this episode were Ellen Holly, John Indrisano, Orlando de la Fuente, Kyle Johnson, Anne Loos, James Healy and Arthur Batanides.

Song: "My Bonnie" (Carter, Schoolchildren)

99. "A Sense of Tempo" May 7, 1964

Dr. Bernard Motley (John Hoyt) who has been author Justin Fitzgibbons' (Cyril Ritchard) doctor for 30 years talks with Gillespie about his patient. Gillespie asks Fitzgibbons, who believes that he is going to die, how he knows that. Claire Sutton (Patricia Crowley), Fitzgibbons' fiancée, tells Kildare about the author. It is Kildare's birthday. Claire later asks Fitzgibbons about her future with the author.

A series of tests is run on Fitzgibbons and they show he is healthy so he is dismissed. The dismissal is brief as the author breaks his left leg just outside Blair.

Writer: Don Balluck

Director: John Newland.

Also featured in this episode were Jeannette Nolan, Nelson Olmsted, Dabney Coleman, Jason Johnson, Ken Drake and Glen Vernon.

100. "Speak Not in Angry Whispers" May 14, 1964

Kildare's newest patient, Hildy Pochek (Lois Nettleton) is suffering from a hearing disorder as well as a kidney ailment.

Kildare and Gus Pochek (Gerald S. O'Laughlin), who works at the hospital, talk about his wife's condition.

Gus finds out that Hildy has been writing poetry for a greeting card company. Hildy survives an operation recommended by Gillespie but Kildare tells Gus that nothing further can be done for her. Hildy tells Kildare that she knows the truth about her condition.

Writer: Edward J. Lakso.

Director: Leo Penn.

Paul Comi, Amanda Ames, James Anderson, Mike Abelar and Peter Virgo also appeared in this episode.

101. "Dolly's Dilemma" May 21, 1964

Gillespie asks Kildare and Lowry for help with Dolly Marlow (Joan Blondell), an old friend of his. She's a widow with a $40 million estate. She also has decided that Gillespie will be her next husband.

Kildare also has a new patient, Tom Monahan (Chester Morris), a Navy veteran who is suffering from a rare parasitical infection. Kildare tells Monahan that his illness can be easily treated with diet and medication.

When Gillespie catches a cold, everyone has remedies. Dolly eventually breaks up with Gillespie and begins a relationship with Monahan, who does an impression of Gillespie.

Writer: Ken Kolb.

Director: John Newland.

Also featured in this episode were Wilton Graff, Alan Hewitt and Lauren Gilbert.

§

Richard Chamberlain and Yvette Mimeux in "Tyger, Tyger."

Chapter 5

The Fourth
TV Season
September 24, 1964
to May 13, 1965

This season opened on September 24, 1964 with Len Wayland joining the cast as Dr. Douglas Lyson. He replaced Ken Berry, who left the show to join the cast of *F Troop* on ABC.

102. "Man Is A Rock" September 24, 1964

Salesman Franklin Gaer, Kildare's newest patient (Walter Matthau), suffers from high blood pressure and refuses to stay in the hospital even though Kildare thinks he's had a heart attack. Gaer goes home where arguments with his wife and daughter (Georgann Johnson, Lana Wood) cause another heart attack.

Kildare tells Gaer that he will need to be in the hospital for at least three weeks. Gaer tries to leave the hospital but is sedated. His second attempt to leave is successful and he goes home. Gillespie tries to warn Gaer from having a meeting with one of his clients but Gaer later changes his mind.

Writer: Christopher Knopf.

Director: Leo Penn.

Richard Evans was also featured in this episode.

103. "Maybe Love Will Save My Apartment House" October 1, 1964

Gillespie asks Kildare for help in finding a husband for his niece Serena Norcross (Suzy Parker). Meanwhile, Kildare gives his parking space to Dr. Wiley Lansing (Barry Nelson) for the day.

Serena invites Lansing to dinner in case her landlord Sylvan Pappinax (Jules Munshin) comes to visit. Lansing later discovers that Dr. Gillespie is Serena's uncle and then asks Kildare about Gillespie's family background. The couple ends up getting married with the wedding being held in Serena's apartment.

Writer: Boris Sobelman.

Director: Ralph Senensky.

Lisa Loring is also featured in this episode.

Medical note: Quincy is the telephone exchange used in the show.

104. "The Hand That Hurts, The Hand That Heals" October 8, 1964

Kildare's newest patient, dress designer Joan Cartwright (Janice Rule), agrees to give him a week to run tests on her. Joan and Annie, another of Kildare's patients (Jeanette Nolan), become friends.

Joan later tries to commit suicide and Kildare uses a blood transfusion to save her life. After more tests, Joan is operated on.

Writer: Edward J. Lakso.

Director: Leo Penn.

Also featured: Steve Ihnat.

Song: "The Trolley Song" (Rule).

105. "The Last Leaves on the Tree" October 15, 1964

When Gillespie returns from a trip, he asks Kildare about his visit to the old Blair mansion. They discuss the motivations of Oliver Blair (Hans Conried) just before a meeting with him.

Blair asks the doctors to a séance to be held by a medium named Miss Plessy at the mansion that evening. At the séance, Amelia (Estelle Winwood) reads her will which includes a provision that Oliver must move to Texas in order to get his share of the estate. It is later revealed that Oliver is not really a Blair.

Writer: Robert Presnell, Jr.

Director: Jack Smight.

Also featured in this episode were Josephine Hutchinson, Edgar Stehli and Burt Mustin.

106. "What's So Different About Today?" October 22, 1964

Kildare serves as the physician at Camp Hocona, a camp for diabetic children. One of them, Sandy Kimball (Kim Darby) falls in love with him and Kildare discusses the situation with Gillespie.

Sandy says she's not worried about her reputation. Kildare tells Sandy that they can only be friends and when she disappears, the camp begins a search for her.

Kildare treats Sandy, who had an insulin reaction and Gillespie talks with her about the disease.

Writer: Jerry McNeely.

Director: Leo Penn.

Patricia Smith and Kelly Corcoran also appeared in this episode.

The sports at camp included archery, golf and swimming.

Songs: "My Darling Clementine," "What's So Different About Today?" (Darby, reprise by Darby and Chamberlain), "My Bonnie" and "Frere Jacques."

107. "The Sound of a Faraway Hill" October 29, 1964

Kildare tells pitcher Buddy Bishop (Lee Marvin), his newest patient, that he is suffering from a heart ailment. Bishop makes friends with Cory Hunter (John Megna), a boy suffering from cystic fibrosis, while Gillespie tells Bishop that he'll never play baseball again.

While Cory is visiting Bishop, Kildare calls Buddy's manager Nate Martin (Ned Glass). Bishop authorizes an operation and Cory awaits the result with his father (David Sheiner). Buddy dies during the operation and Hunter buys a pair of ball gloves for himself and his son.

Writers: Don Tait and Edward J. Lakso.

Director: Alf Kjellin.

108. "A Candle in the Window" November 5, 1964

Kildare wonders why Lily Prentice (Ruth Roman), a nurse at Blair, is back at work the day after her husband's funeral. After her son Jerry (Ron Howard) falls asleep, she calls a neighbor to look after him and then goes to the hotel where she and her husband Mike spent their honeymoon.

Gillespie later asks Fain about Lily's behavior. When Lily asks Kildare why he didn't spend more time with Mike when he was alive, Kildare asks about Lily's trips to the hotel. During one of her visits, customer Joe Filsch comes to her room and goes into convulsions and Lily calls Kildare for help. Lily takes a leave of absence after a talk with Gillespie.

Writer: Rita Lakin.
Director: Sydney Pollack.
Eddie Firestone was also featured in this episode.
Song: "How Dry I Am."

*109-111. "Rome Will Never Leave You" November 2, 19 and 26, 1964

Daniela Bianchi, a Bond girl in *From Russia with Love,* made her American TV debut in this three-part story in which both Kildare and Gillespie find romance. Also featured in the episode arc were Donald Harron, Fabrizio Mioni, Mercedes McCanbridge, Ramon Novarro, Paul Stewart, Alida Valli, Anna Bruno-Lena, Teresa Tirelli and Mimi Aguglia.

Writers: Jane and Ira Avery, Sally Benson.
Director: John Newland.

112. "The Elusive Dik-Dik" December 9, 1964

Foster Bailey (Tom Helmore), an expert on tropical diseases, is suffering from blurred vision and fever. Kildare gets help on the case from Jesse Kimba, also an expert on the subject, and his wife, a laboratory technician (Bill Gunn, Barbara McNair).

The Kimbas discover the illness is not contagious, but it is fatal, and think Bailey may have caught it during a visit to the zoo. They discover that the dik-dik, a miniature antelope, is the cause of the infection which has now infected Brian Bailey (Michel Petit).

Kildare and Bailey discuss the case as well as deciding which patients to help. Kildare and Gillespie disagree on whom should get the serum, Bailey or his son. Despite getting a dose of the serum, Bailey dies and the doctors must tell Brian.

Writer: Barry Lyndon.
Director: John Newland.
Geraldine Brooks, Nelson Olmsted and Vic Perrin are also featured in this episode.

113. "Catch a Crooked Mouse" December 17, 1964

Kathryn Lambert, Kildare's newest patient, is dying of a heart condition. She is also a potential witness against Nick Buchanan (Joe Maross), her brother-in-law, in a case being handled by Assistant DA John Bardeman (Andrew Prine).

When the Buchanans arrive, Kildare assigns Lowry to keep Buchanan from bothering his sister-in-law. He also denies Bardeman permission to see Lambert, who dies shortly thereafter. The Buchanans argue after that and his wife says she never wants to see him again.

Writer: Stanley Niss.

Director: Boris Sagal.

Medical advisor: Dr. Walter Swanson took over that job as of this episode, which also featured Harold J. Stone, Fay Spain, Joe Mantell and Milton Frome.

114. "An Exchange of Gifts" December 24, 1964

John Burroughs (Rip Torn), Kildare's newest patient, breaks a bottle of brandy that Kildare meant to give Gillespie as a Christmas gift. Gillespie's office is the setting for the Blair Christmas party.

The other patients on his ward confront Burroughs when he demands the student nurses stop singing Christmas carols. Kildare picks up a package for Burroughs that was left in his apartment.

Gillespie's Christmas gift to Kildare is the first edition of a classic medical text. Meanwhile, Burroughs starts a riot in the ward by tossing a huge sum of cash around, which he later demands back. A patient named Callahan (John Qualen) helps Kildare get most of the money back. After Kildare confronts Burroughs about his selfishness, he makes a large donation to the hospital.

Writers: Irving Pearlberg and Robert Lewin.

Director: Richard Sarafian.

Bern Bassey is also featured in this episode, during which the following songs are performed: "Silent Night," "The First Noel", "Joy to the World" and "Have Yourself a Merry Little Christmas."

115. "Never Is A Long Day" December 31, 1964

Dr. Max Jurgens (Walter Slezak), an old friend of Gillespie's, is suffering from a terminal illness and Gillespie assigns Kildare to look after him. Jurgens is concerned about his wife Gretl (Hanna Lundy) and asks Gillespie how he copes with being a widower.

Jurgens later drugs Gretl and nearly commits suicide by walking into the ocean with her in his arms, but changes his mind. Kildare reveals her husband's condition to Gretl, who decides to visit her sister in Vienna.

Writers: Rita Lakin, Margaret and Paul Schneider.

Director: Leo Penn.

Irene Tedrow and Marge Redmond were also featured.

116. "Lullaby for an Indian Summer" January 7, 1965

Dr. Gilbert Winfield (Robert Young), Blair's chief of obstetrics, is about to become a father again. Mrs. Winfield (Margaret Leighton) is suffering from a kidney disorder.

Kildare examines Winfield but it is Gillespie who has to tell his old friend that he has at most, a year more to live, and Winfield keeps that from his wife. Fain tells Kildare how Winfield is treating his staff and Gillespie suggests that Winfield retire.

Writer: Jameson Brewer.

Director: Herschel Daugherty.

Also featured: Tisha Sterling.

Medical note: David Victor, who served as both producer and supervising producer on Dr. Kildare, would work again with Robert Young on another medical show, *Marcus Welby, M.D.*

117. "Take Care of My Little Girl" January 14, 1965

Nancy Hiller (Veronica Cartwright) is brought to Blair for observation after an accident at her school. Kildare and Dr. Milton Bremner are assigned her case.

Eddie Hiller (Larry Blyden) suggests suing the school where Nancy was injured to his wife Helen (Gail Kobe). He brings gifts to Nancy while Kildare is called to pathology where Gillespie says one of Nancy's legs must be amputated because of a malignant tumor.

Hiller is told by Nancy to leave her alone when she discovers her condition. When he returns, he goes to the roof and considers committing suicide until Kildare says he must not care much for his family. After Nancy leaves the hospital, Hiller takes a job with record store owner Dave Lesser (Stuart Erwin).

Writers: Irving Pearlberg, Beryl Kent.

Director: Alf Kjellin.

118. "My Name is Lisa and I Am Lost" January 21, 1965

Georgia Pettigrew (Nina Foch), Kildare's newest patient, claims she has an ulcer and demands to see Gillespie. Kildare takes Lisa Dowling (Lois Nettleton), a new nurse, to lunch at Mac's and tries to boost her self-confidence. Meanwhile, Pettigrew complains about Lisa to Gillespie.

After Kildare takes Lisa home after a shift, she and her Aunt Martha (Carmen Matthews) have an argument. Lisa leaves Blair after Pettigrew acts rudely to her. The investigation of the incident by an investigator named McCoy proves Pettigrew is a fraud but Lisa admits to giving her a black eye. She decides to leave home so she can live her own life

Writers: James F. Griffith, James Thompson.

Director: Jud Taylor.

119. "Please Let My Baby Live" January 28, 1965

Marguerite Williams (Diana Hyland), a nurse who formerly worked at Blair, and Kildare reminiscence before the arrival of her husband Paul (Peter Haskell). After giving sedatives to Williams and her roommate Clara McCloskey (Marge Redmond), Kildare asks Williams how she feels.

Kildare finds out that Marguerite won't consider adoption even though her pregnancies have been difficult. Gillespie and Kildare discuss the case as the Williams baby is delivered.

Kildare and Mrs. McCloskey join Paul in looking at the baby, who has been named Michael Paul Williams. The baby later dies. The McCloskeys, who now have six daughters, visit briefly with Marguerite before they leave the hospital.

Writer: Max Hodge.

Director: Leo Penn.

Harold Gould, Pauline Myers and Peggy Rea also appear in this episode. Kildare also shows a talent for composing the first two lines of five-line limericks, reciting this one:

There was a young nurse from Duluth,
Who got drunk on gin and vermouth.

*120. "No Mother to Guide Them" February 4, 1965

Writer: Adrian Spies.

Director: John Newland.

Guest stars in this episode were Jack Warden, Patricia Hyland, Adrienne Hayes, Joan Tompkins, Bill Quinn, Richard Angarola, Richard Wessel and Jonathan Lippe.

*121. "A Marriage of Convenience" February 11, 1965

Writers: Agnes Ridgway and Don Balluck.

Guest stars in this episode were Burt Brinckerhoff, Louise Sorel, Audrey Christie, Maidie Norman, Stephen Perry Jr., Shelley Morrison, Rodolfo Hoyos and Joey Russo.

122. "Make Way for Tomorrow" February 18, 1965

Kildare and Lowry discuss his newest patient, a former merchant seaman named Jamie Cousins (Ed Begley) who owns a ship named the Sara Lee, Hannah Lacey (Mabel Albertson), a social worker, is assigned Cousins' case and finds him a job.

Fain tells Lowry and Kildare that Cousins is giving the staff problems. After examining the seaman, Kildare takes away Cousins' hospital gown.

Lowry delivers a letter to Cousins which reveals that his boat was destroyed in a fire. When Cousins leaves the hospital, he takes a job at a museum in Maine.

Writer: E. Arthur Kean.

Director: Herschel Daugherty.

Also featured in this episode were Joanna Barnes and Frank Puglia.

123. "A Miracle for Margaret" February 25, 1965

When an old friend dies under his care, Kildare confronts Dr. Ruth Halliman (Barbara Bel Geddes) about whether an autopsy is necessary or not. He then asks to have tests done to determine if his new patient, Margaret Beaton, has leukemia.

Kildare meets with Dr. Arthur Untermeyer (Ford Rainey) about his research into the disease. Halliman and Kildare examine slides of his friend's autopsy. Halliman then gives Margaret, whose nickname is Mardy, a book of poetry and discovers that Kildare has not started treating her yet.

Gillespie thinks Mardy may have aplastic anemia and not leukemia. Kildare decides to stay in internal medicine.

Writers: Dr. Arthur L. Murphy and Irving Pearlberg.

Director: John Newland.

Phyllis Hill, Nina Shipman and Richard O'Brien also appeared in this episode.

*124. "Do You Trust Your Doctor?" March 4, 1965

Writers: Chester Krumholz and Jerry MacNeely.

Director: Leo Penn.

Featured in this episode about a doctor who is reluctant to treat patients after losing a malpractice suit were Robert Culp, Angie Dickinson, Leslie Nielsen, Jason Wingreen, Loretta Leversee, George Cisar, Carol Anderson and Alma Pratt.

125. "All Brides Should Be Beautiful" March 11, 1965

Eleanor Markham (Colleen Dewhurst), an old friend of Kildare's, has a lump in her breast and Kildare watches with Gillespie while a biopsy is taken. Gillespie tells Eleanor that she needs a mastectomy. She refuses to tell her husband Harry (Tom Bosley) about her condition.

Eleanor later reveals how she felt about Kildare during their college days. She begins radiation therapy but decides to undergo the mastectomy when she finds out that she's pregnant.

Writer: Edward J. Lakso.

Director: Alf Kjellin.

Connie Gilchrist and Rusty Lane were also featured in this episode.

126 and 127. "She Loves Me. She Loves Me Not" March 18 and 25, 1965

Kildare is badly hurt in an auto accident during his second date with Carol Tredman (Angie Dickinson). Gillespie supervises Kildare's treatment and asks him about his feelings for Tredman. He has both of them put on his service where Kildare has nightmares about the accident.

Tredman recognizes Dr. Thomas Eastly (James McMullan) as the man who fled the scene after the accident and confronts him. Eastly confesses his actions to Gillespie just before he resigns. Meanwhile, Carol is visited by Walter Burton (Leslie Nielsen), who later tells Kildare that Carol is a liar and cheat.

Kildare, who has proposed to Carol, says he doesn't care about her past and only cares if they have a future together.

Writer: Jerry McNeely.

Director: Leo Penn.

Trivia: The pianist in the nightclub scene during this two-parter is Marvin Hamlisch. Also featured in this episode is Robert Hogan.

*128. "A Journey to the Sunrise" April 1, 1965

Massey plays a dual role in this episode as Gillespie and Graham Lanier, a new patient at Blair, who refuses to reveal anything about himself. Also featured in this episode are Malcolm Atterbury, Ellen Atterbury, Don Quine, William Arvin and Teddy Eccles.

Writer: Jack Curtis.

Director: Ralph Senensky.

129. "The Time Buyers" April 8, 1965

Gillespie tells Dr. Edith Burnside (Patricia Barry) that her son Alan (Roger Mobley) may be suffering from a kidney ailment but that there are new treatments that could save him, including a kidney transplant.

Dr. Burnside reveals that her husband David (Carroll O'Connor) is not the boy's father and that his biological father, Chris McKenna (Donnelly Rhodes), a school athletic director, is the only possible donor. McKenna, however, refuses to help at first but changes his mind just before he leaves to take a new job.

Writers: Herbert A. Spiro, Archie Lawrence and Max Hodge.

Director: John Newland.

Evelyn Ward, Les Tremayne, Jeannine Rainier, Pauline Myers and Marian Moses are also featured in this episode.

130. "Music Hath Charms" April 15, 1965

Composer Harlan Thomas (Daryl Hickman), a hypochondriacal patient at Blair, is drafted by Kildare to help with the hospital's annual variety show. Gillespie gives the hospital's fifth floor solarium to Kildare for rehearsals.

Judge Angela Faring (Rosemary DeCamp), an old friend of Gillespie's, refuses to sign a surgical release unless he sings a song composed by Thomas for her in the show. Gillespie reluctantly agrees.

Dr. Kline (Whit Bissell) has to tell Gillespie that his friend died during the surgery. Gillespie still sings the song as a tribute to his friend.

Writer: Edward J. Lakso

Director: Sidney Miller.

Also featured in the episode were Dorothy Provine, William Splawn, Karen Dolin, Rita D'Amico and Jimmy Murphy.

The songs used in the episode were composed by Lakso, Burton Lane, Ralph Freed, Nicholas Brodksy and Sammy Cahn. The featured songs: "How About You?" (Chamberlain, Provine); "Lovebirds" (D'Amico, Murphy and Tim Herbert); "Once Before You Go" (Hickman with reprise by Massey); "Now, Baby, Now" (Chamberlain, Provine), and "Bachelor Doctors" (Bell, Taylor, Herbert, Dolin)

131. "Believe and Live" April 22, 1965

Attorney Mark Sloan (Dan O'Herlihy), a specialist in medical law, is brought to Blair after passing out at a party. When his wife arrives, Sloan tries to question Kildare about his condition.

The doctors discuss the case just before Gillespie gets Sloan's test results. Gillespie sees Sloan in the recovery room, just before he leaves on a trip to Chicago and Kildare tells Sloan there is nothing wrong with him. However, Sloan insists on getting a second opinion.

Writers: Toby and Dr. Marshall Goldberg, Boris Sobelman.

Director: John Newland.

Also featured in this episode are Kevin McCarthy, Anne Jeffreys and Conrad Nagel.

132. "A Reverence for Life" April 29. 1965

A car driven by Kildare strikes Ruth Wandermeer (Phyllis Love) during a rainstorm while she is on the way home from the neighborhood pharmacy. Her husband Wayne (Dennis Weaver) tells Gillespie and Kildare that their religion does not permit blood transfusions: Mr. Wandermeer thinks she should do it anyway. Ruth rejects the idea.

Gillespie discusses the situation with hospital attorney Vincent Thompson (Norman Fell) before a meeting with Judge Reynolds. Reynolds refuses to issue an order requiring the transfusion. Kildare, who disagrees with the decision, orders a transfusion after Ruth loses consciousness.

Writer: Archie L. Tegland.

Director: Jud Taylor.

Frank Maxwell and Ron Husmann were also featured in this episode.

*133. "Wings of Hope" May 13, 1965

This last original episode in the time slot the show had occupied for four seasons concerned an airline pilot, Capt. Bob Hill (Earl Holliman) whose career is over if he is diagnosed with asthma. Also appearing in the episode were Sharon Farrell, Sally Chamberlain and Whit Bissell.

Writers: Dr. Harold Kaiser, Max Hodge.

Director: John Newland.

§

Raymond Massey.

Chapter 6

The Final
TV Season
September 13, 1965
to April 5, 1966

T he show returned to its roots for its final season on NBC as the original Max Brand stories had been serialized in magazines such as *Argosy* and *Cosmopolitan*. The stories ran from two to eight parts and the show was aired on Mondays and Tuesdays at 8:30 p.m. EST.

The writer and director of each story will appear at the end of each arc as will the actors appearing in it besides the principal co-stars. New regulars joining the show cast were Lee Kurty, Jeff Donnell, James Seay, Cynthia Stone and Susan Silo.

134. "Behold the Great Man" September 13, 1965

Kildare clashes with surgeon Maxwell Becker (James Mason) about a surgery that caused the death of an elderly patient. Kildare had talked with the patient, Molly Lindemann, about how she wanted to end her life.

When a burn victim named Charlie Shannon (Burt Brinckerhoff) comes in a week later, Kildare thinks Becker is the best surgeon for the case, and assigns Gerson to help him. Kildare later witnesses an argument between Becker and his wife (Margaret Leighton), who is drunk.

135. "A Life for A Life" September 14, 1965

Gerson and Kildare spent the night at Shannon's bedside with Kildare telling Shannon the church where he was found is in the same condition he is. Gillespie tells Kildare that Becker has been paralyzed in a car accident and faces renal failure. Shannon asks Gillespie if he believes in God while Becker considers his future, which he says may involve teaching.

Becker's chauffeur Garcia (Rodolfo Hoyos) brings a gun along with some papers that Becker has asked for. Gillespie gives Becker a redwood whistle as a good luck piece. Kildare offers to help Becker after finding him with the gun.

136. "Web of Hate" September 20. 1965

Two patients, Mrs. Gast and Mrs. Anderson (Naomi Stevens, Sara Haden), talk about Becker's treatment while the doctors wonder why Becker is throwing his wife and Kildare together. Shannon asks the doctors how Becker is doing while Gillespie tells Kildare people are talking about him and the Beckers.

While being examined by Becker, Shannon admits to setting the church where he was found on fire. Becker says surgery on Shannon can wait for two weeks.

137. "Horizontal Hero" September 21, 1965

When a priest comes to see Shannon, he orders him away. Becker says he'll operate on Shannon, but also thinks Shannon needs psychiatric help. During the operation, Becker uses a device similar to a barber's chair.

The Beckers consider divorce, but decide to stay together. Shannon decides to turn himself in after the surgery and Mrs. Gast says she'll stay with him to find out the results of the operation.

Writer: Adrian Spies.
Director: John Brahm.
Also featured were Robert Cornthwaite, Catherine Weeks, Kim Hamilton, John Lodge and Mark Vance.

138. "The Bell in the Schoolhouse Tolls for Thee, Kildare"
   September 27, 1965

With help from his teaching assistant Roger Helvick (Andrew Prine) is in charge of training three new interns. They are Tom Hartwood (Tony Bill), Rudy Devereux (Dean Stockwell) and Frankie Warren (Sheilah Wells).

Kildare explains the interns' schedule to them while Gillespie explains his role in their training.

139. "Life in the Dance Hall: F-U-N" September 28, 1965

Helvick (Andrew Prine) wakes Kildare up from a bad dream and later accuses him of playing footsy with Gillespie during a talk with Deveraux.

One of Kildare's patients, Mr. Cooper, doesn't want a woman doctor handling him because he is having a colostomy and later confesses a fear of the unpleasant aspects of medicine to Kildare.

140. "Some Doors Are Slamming" October 5, 1965

Gillespie joins Kildare and his students on their rounds. Warren (aids Dr. Bernard Krantz while Helvick, who's supposed to aid Hartwood with an IV, ducks the job. Helvick talks about Gillespie behind his back after Gillespie criticizes him for botching a procedure

Dr. Hartwood and his wife argue about their home life after he finds her on the phone with her mother.

141. "Enough La Boheme for Everybody" October 11, 1965

Lawton finds that Helvick has used pills himself that he was supposed to give a patient. When Gillespie finds out, he asks for Helvick's resignation.

Kildare finds Cairns arguing with Warren about her talents or lack thereof. Hartwood later faces an ultimatum from his wife—give up medicine or her—and he tells her to leave.

142. "Now the Mummy" October 12, 1965

Devereux engineers a protest over what Helvick calls his firing until Kildare explains what really happened. Meanwhile, Kildare gets a new patient and Hartwood tells Wheeler that he's separated from his wife.

143. "A Pyrotechnic Display" October 18, 1965

When a patient dies, Warren decides to give up medicine. Gillespie discusses new cases with a distracted Kildare and he goes to see Warren, telling her that nobody could have saved that patient.

Lawton dislikes Mrs. Stephenson, a new patient, while the Hartwoods discuss their situation. Gillespie joins Kildare and his interns on their rounds.

Writer: Jerry De Bono.

Director: Jud Taylor (who played Dr. Gerson).

Also featured were Judy Lang, Ariane Quinn, Marjorine Bennety, Tim Rooney and Murray Rose.

Trivia: Sam Waterston of *Law and Order* plays a bit part as a teacher.

144. "With Hellfire and Thunder" October 19, 1965

Kildare and Gillespie both think something more is involved when actor Morgan Bannion (James Daly) calls for a routine physical. Bannion tells his assistant MacAllister Thane (Sorrell Booke) that he believes he has cancer but it turns out to be a liver ailment.

The doctors tell Bannion's wife Madge (Barbara Rush) that he could die unless the ailment is properly treated. The couple later reminisces about their past.

145. "Daily Flights to Olympus" October 25, 1965

Bannion is found by Kildare in a bar where he's causing a disturbance. He brings Bannion to Blair for treatment for injuries caused by three men who beat him up.

Kildare goes to the Bannion home where he finds Madge in the garden. They discuss Bannion's character and the doctors later discuss how to treat Bannion.

Writer: Christopher Knopf.

Director: Jud Taylor.

Also featured in this story are Bert Freed, James Dawson, Audrey Larkin, George Savalas and Marrisa Mathes.

146. "The Life Machine" October 26, 1965

Dr. Wickens' invention, an artificial kidney, is being tested on Harry Kleber (Leslie Nielsen). Gillespie is in charge of a committee of doctors and laymen who will decide who will be treated. When Nurse Fain shows Kildare some of the equipment to be used, she says she wants another assignment.

147. "Toast the Golden Couple" November 1, 1965

Judd Morrison (Robert Reed), an old friend of Kildare's, tries to get on the list. He and his wife Laura (Marlyn Mason) give Kildare a book on medicine by Leonardo da Vinci as Gillespie watches.

Fred Kirsh and Mitchell Hobart (David Opatoshu, Fred Scollay) discuss their situations regarding the machine while their wives Rhoda (Cloris Leachman) and Norma (Hazel Court) visit in the hospital lobby.

148. "Wives and Losers" November 2, 1965

Gillespie shows the committee members (Edmon Ryan, Karl Swenson, Hayden Rorke, James Edwards and Mrs. Canford) the machine while three families hoping they can get members on it visit in Blair's solarium.

The committee begins creating selection criteria while one candidate, Morrison, leaves the hospital. An angry Steve Perrona (Tom Nardini), whose wife Anna is a candidate for the machine, starts a fight with Kildare that Kleber has to break up.

149. "Welcome Home, Dear Anna" November 8, 1965

Morrison tells Kildare that Laura is an alcoholic and Gillespie says he knows about it, too. Anna is back home and wants to fix dinner for her family but reveals to her husband that she knows about her condition.

Gillespie discusses Nurse Fain, who wants her husband to go on the machine with Kildare. Kildare also has a talk with Morrison. Laura arrives just before Kildare leaves, saying that she missed her husband.

150. "A Little Child Shall Lead" November 9, 1965

Perrona tries to offer Gillespie a bribe of $1,000 to put his wife on the kidney machine but he returns it. After he does so, Mrs. Perrona tells Gillespie off.

After Wickens (Philip Bourneuf) and Kildare discuss Kleber's situation with him, Fain reveals what she knows about Kleber, who leaves the hospital with his girlfriend.

While Kirsh and Hobart discuss their family situations, Kirsh's daughter Harriet (Suzanne Cupito) comes to see Kildare, who's getting ready for a date. Hobart asks Kirsh if having a job would help him get on the machine.

Trivia: Young actress Suzanne Cupito would later change her name to Morgan Brittany, and would remain a modeling and acting force for years to come, best remembered for her work on *Dallas*.

151. "Hour of Decision" November 15, 1965

Kildare gives Gillespie his report on Morrison just before the committee assembles to make their decisions on who will get on the life machine. Wickens makes his report to the committee.

Fain and Lawton look at the life machine list. Morrison and Kildare talk outside the life machine and Laura confronts Kildare until Judd stops her.

152. "Aftermath" November 16, 1965

Gillespie talks to the five persons chosen for treatment with Kildare and Fain supervising the process. When Kleber, one of those picked, doesn't show up for treatment, Kildare begins searching for him.

Kleber has gone to the country club after a long day at work. He is drunk when he checks into a flophouse and calls the Perronas and gives up his machine slot to Mrs. Perrona.

Writer: Jerome Ross.

Director: Marc Daniels.

Also featured in this arc were Victor French, Elizabeth Rogers, Joan Granville and Dennis King Jr.

153. "Fathers and Daughters" November 22, 1965

Kildare talks with Sister Benjamin (Laura Devon) about her illness while Gillespie talks with his old friend, Mother Caritas (Spring Byington) on whether Sister Benjamin should receive a bone marrow transplant.

Sister Benjamin gives a lecture attended by among others, Kildare and her father Joe Quinlan (Fred Astaire), who's also a pool hustler. Also at the lecture are Sister Benjamin's aunt and uncle, Ella and Arnold Vilsack (Audrey Totter, Norman Fell.)

Kildare tells Quinlan that tests show that his daughter has stem cell leukemia. Quinlan and Sister Benjamin later talk about his life and he asks her why she's at Blair instead of a Catholic hospital. Sister Benjamin discovers that Quinlan has a heart condition for which he's taking nitroglycerin.

154. "A Gift of Love" November 13, 1965

The Vitnacks visit Gillespie about Quinlan's condition while Kildare discovers that he has been invited to compete in a pool tournament. Francis X. Healy (Harry Morgan) and Quinlan watch Healy's former boxer Luther Bernstein (James Frawley) go through rehabilitation.

Ella, Quinlan's sister, brings him a book and a box of candy for Luther on one of her visits. Sister Benjamin talks with candy striper Tracey Richards (Kathy Garver) about her boyfriend. A patient named Gaffney (Alan Hewitt) challengers Healy to a game of pool but Healy turns him down but tells Quinlan that he'd be a perfect patsy for the pro.

155. "The Tent-Dwellers" November 24, 1965

Fain covers for Lawton, who's searching for Quinlan. He and Gaffney are in the hospital's recreation room playing pool with Healy making side bets with the greedy Gaffney before Lawton finds them.

Kildare and Sister Banjamin talk about Quinlan, including how much longer he has to live. Fain asks about Sister Benjamin while Gillespie goes to see Quinlan, who reports on how Bernstein is doing.

156. "Going Home" November 30, 1965

Healy tells Gillespie that he had nothing to do with Quinlan's escape. He is one of the competitors in an international pool tournament with Kildare and Healy among the spectators.

Vitnack comes in just as Quinlan misses a shot. However, he wins his match just before he collapses. Sister Banjamin, who is now in remission, goes to see her father when he returns to the hospital. When Quinlan dies, Sister Benjamin asks Luther for his pool cue.

Writer: William Fay.

Director: Herschel Daugherty.

Also appearing in this arc were James Flavin, Harold Baker and Jan Arvan.

Trivia: A padded stool was kept on the set for Astaire.

157. "Something Old, Something New" December 6, 1965

Rachel Field (Sharon Farrell) and Terry Cole are injured in an accident and Terry later dies. When Rachel becomes hysterical, Gillespie orders that she be medicated.

Rachel tells Lawton that she and Terry were on their way to get married at the time of the accident. Gillespie tells Rachel's mother (Kim Hunter) that her daughter is suffering from a form of lymphoma and has less than a year to live. Later on, Rachel winds up comforting her mother.

158. "To Visit One More Spring" December 7, 1965

Kildare and Rachel argue in the hospital pharmacy about her plans for the baby. She's taking medication instead of receiving radiation therapy. Rachel's mother gives her a gift and Kildare later asks her out for her 21st birthday. She uses the dress Terry gave her.

Mrs. Fields asks Kildare what will happen to Rachel's baby and Kildare says the baby will be up for adoption, unless Mrs. Fields decides to keep it.

Writers: Edward J. Lakso, Darlene E. Kardon.

Director: John Brahm.

159. "From Nigeria with Love" December 13, 1965

Felix Holman (Darren McGavin), an anthropologist and an old friend of Gillespie's, is brought to Blair for treatment. His companion is a missionary named Lydia McGuire (Patricia Barry).

Kildare visits in the cafeteria with Lois Gibbon, who has just dropped out of college, and he agrees to get her a job in the laboratory. Kildare and Dr. Stan Brantell discuss how to treat Holman. He goes into convulsions after being put on a new drug.

160. "In the Roman Candle's Bright Glare" December 14, 1965

Lawton finds Holman and McGuire arguing when she delivers a package from Africa to him. Gillespie reads Kildare a letter which Holman got from the village where he lived in Africa.

Lois and McGuire visit in the hospital cafeteria where Lois asks McGuire if she loves Holman or not. When Kildare asks Lois for a date, she turns him down.

161. "When Shadows Fall" December 20, 1965

Kildare tells Gillespie his plans for treating Holman just before McGuire comes for a talk with him. Lois runs away from the hospital when she is fired but her boss tells Kildare that he'll give her a second chance.

Tests that Kildare run for Holman's backache reveal that the man has a terminal kidney condition.

162. "With This Ring" December 21, 1965

Holman is dictating his new book to McGuire and later asks Kildare how much longer he has to live. Kildare tells McGuire that Holman's cancer has metastasized and she later brings him a big box of chocolates.

When Holman proposes marriage to McGuire, she accepts. Later on, Lois tells Kildare that she is quitting her job and returning to college. The doctors take McGuire to the airport after Holman's death.

Writer: Meyer Dolinsky.

Director: Michael Ritchie.

Also featured in this arc were Robert F. Simon, Tippy Walker and William Sargent.

Song: "I've Been Working on the Railroad" (McGavin).

Trivia: Three stuffed animal heads are on a wall of Holman's hospital room.

163. "Perfect Is Too Hard to Be" December 27, 1965

When Dr. Jessie Martel (Susan Oliver) freezes up, Kildare as to do a lumbar puncture for her, Lawton and Kildare go to Mac's after their shift ends. Gillespie later talks with Kildare about Martel.

Annie Foray, an old friend of Gillespie's, comes to visit and they discuss her husband Frederick (Basil Rathbone), a musician who blames Gillespie for their daughter's death. The two men later visit and Gillespie observes Foray's health. Foray then asks for Gillespie's health. Martel is assigned to the case and she argues with Foray about his interpretation of Chopin.

164. "Duet for One Hand" December 28, 1965

Foray is suffering from Parkinson's disease and the doctors discuss his case. His son Philip asks Foray about a concert schedule and Martel orders him out of the room. Gillespie tells Foray that surgery could aid him and he agrees to an operation.

Dr. Norman Hobbs, the dean of Ames Medical School, tells Kildare that Martel flunked out and Gillespie confronts her about her actions. Foray asks to see Martel, and then thanks Gillespie for his efforts. Kildare suggests that Martel could help Foray.

Writer: John W. Block.

Director: Alf Kjellin.

Also featured in this story arc were Frances Reid, Ronald Long, David Frankham, Robert Karnes and Russell Collins.

165. "The Atheist and the True Believer" January 3, 1966

Evangelist Abdrew Webb and Justin Post, an avowed atheist (Bradford Dillman, Jack Hawkins). discuss their views after Webb's tour of Blair. Gillespie and Post talk about Post is planning.

Kildare and Bryan Cannon (Donald Madden) discuss the need for brain surgery with Mrs. Cannon (Joyce Bulifant) talking with Kildare before going to see her husband.

Post collapses after his daughter Amy (Diana Baker) tells him that she is staying in California. Kildare and Lawton are assigned his case when he is brought to Blair.

166. "A Quick Look at Glory" January 4, 1966

Post does not want any visitors. A newspaper implies that Webb said Post's heart attack was a punishment from God. Amy is among those who see the story while Post says that he saw God.

Kildare and Cannon discuss the story and Cannon's beliefs. Webb and Amy talk in Gillespie's office.

167. "A Sort of Falling in Love" January 10. 1966

The doctors discuss Post's condition and Post tells Lawton that he wants to see Dr. Webb. Kildare and Amy discuss her father and his newfound belief in God but Gillespie believes that Post's experience may have a physical cause.

168. "The Last to Believe in Miracles" January 11, 1966

Post wants to Join Webb in his work. Kildare says Post needs bed rest until he's completely healed. Amy asks Kildare to publicly announce his belief that Post is mentally ill. Kildare refuses but agrees that Post is not up to any public appearances. Mrs. Cannon talks with Gillespie about her husband.

169. "The Next Thing to Murder" January 17, 1966

Gillespie says that Kildare making any announcement about Post would be a violation of medical ethics. Cannon tells the doctors why he agreed to being operated on.

Rev. Kenneth Cleveland and Webb argue over his plans to put Post on television. Amy and her father discuss his condition while Post reveals why Amy came home to Kildare.

170. "Never So Happy" January 18, 1966

Post talks with the Cannons on his way to his TV appearance with Webb. Amy tells Kildare that she's returning to her magazine job.

Cleveland tells Webb that he's leaving his organization just before the telecast. During his appearance, Post tells about his memories and even mentions Kildare's theory of brain damage. He has another heart attack right after the broadcast. He still believes in God and tells Amy so.

Writers: Jerry McNeely and Rik Vollaerts
Director: Herschel Daugherty
Also appearing in this arc are Len Wayland and John Napier.

171. "A Cry from the Street" January 24, 1966

A fight breaks out between strikers and workers at the Metropolitan Produce Market. At the scene, Dr Louis Rush (James Earl Jones) helps a policeman find two injured men under a large number of crates while Kildare is called to Blair's emergency and to help with the injuries expected.

Rush visits with his sister Irene (Diana Sands) and his brother Jerry in the elevator while taking Jerry to Kildare's ward. Irene invites Kildare to dinner. Kildare and Gillespie visit with Dr. Denarest about four men suffering from the same ailment. Gillespie offers Rush a residency at Blair.

172. "Gratitude Won't Pay the Bills" January 25, 1966

Irene takes Kildare to a bar owned by the family where a gang harasses a woman named Alice (Beah Richards) until Irne chases them out with a baseball bat.

Jerry goes to visit his friend Pappas (Eduardo Ciannelli), who wants him to help his siblings and stay in school. Kildare finds them arguing and orders Jerry to return to his room.

Demarest thinks the disease is caused by the ingestion of lead while Irene visits George Parker in the jail ward and he asks for a loan.

173. "Adrift in A Sea of Confusion" January 31, 1966

Kildare and Rush discuss Alice and the disease while Alice is being watched by the gang that harassed her at the bar. They find her cache of money in an old car.

After Jerry id dismissed. he then goes to see Pappas and joins Lawton in listening to his tales of Greece. Pappas passes ouf after doing a dance of his homeland. After Pappas' death, Jerry meets the gang.

Irene tells Rush and Kildare that a badly injured Alice is at Blair and she later dies from her injuries. Jerry tells Kildare that he knos what happened to Alice anbd her money.

174. "These Hands That Heal" February 1, 1966

Jerry leads his brother and Kildare to Alice's home where they find her still, the cause of the ailment. Jerry is being hunted by the gang. The doctors find them and then Jerry, who is sitting by Pappas' casket. The Rush brothers reconcile.

When the doctors go to Irene's bar, they find one of the bottles from Alice's still. Kildare confronts Irene about her actions while Rush smashes the bottles.

Song: "We Are So Few" is part of the arc's musical score, which was composed by Lalo Schifrin, who wrote the theme for Mission: Impossible.

Writer: Edward L. Lakso.

Director: Corey Allen.

Also featured in this arc were Barry Atwater, John Perrow, Rupert Crosse and Bill Zuckert.

175. "A Few Hearts, A Few Flowers" February 7, 1966

Writer Damon West (Ricardo Montalban) tries to commit suicide by taking drugs but changes his mind and takes a cab to Blair. He passes out in Gillespie's office and Gillespie tells his wife (Elizabeth Allen) about West's actions.

Gillespie and Peter De Gravio (Edward Binns) talk about how to raise funds for the hospital. Meanwhile, Kildare examines Bonda Jo Weaver (Lesley Ann Warren), who's about to have a baby.

176. "Some Tales for Halloween" February 8, 1966
Gillespie has a heart attack. Meanwhile, Bonda Jo wakes up to find her husband has left her and Kildare breaks up another argument between the Wests. West later tells Lawton how he became a writer.

Kildare tells West that he needs to see a psychiatrist before he leaves. Weaver returns home to find a note from his wife. Bonda later goes into labor and later says she doesn't want the baby.

177. "I Can Hear the Ice Melting" February 14, 1966
Kildare talks with Paul Lee about his new baby boy. West gives Lawton a manuscript to read just before Kildare and Lawton reconcile. Gillespie tells Kildare that he wants to retire and asks him to set up a meeting with DeGravio.

Kildare tries to talk Gillespie out of his decision while West asks Lawton to come to his apartment.

178. "No Other Road" February 15, 1966
Kildare and Zoe's roommate Angie are playing cards when she returns to their apartment. After asking about her meeting with West, Kildare asks Lawton for a date. The Weavers decide to keep their baby and Gillespie decides not to resign.

Mrs. West calls her marriage a symbiosis when the couple discusses their situation. Lawton keeps her date with West and finds another girl there.

Writer: Jerry De Bono.
Director: Herschel Daughterty.
Music score: Lyn Murray.
Song: "Walk Down Lonesome Road" (Massey, Steve Carlson).

179. "The Encroachment" February 21, 1966
Yvonne Barlow (Joanna Pettet) tells Dr. Milton Orloff, a fellow patient (Martin Balsam) and Kildare that she wants Kildare for her doctor and not Dr. Carl Noyes (William Shatner). Noyes calls Orloff a nuisance later.

Barlow later admits that she may be a hypochondriac but says that Noyes is an emotional cripple. Kildare meets Orloff's wife (Diana Muldaur) and daughter and discovers that the little girl is deaf. After he has an attack, Orloff offers to sell his practice to Kildare and Noyes.

180. "A Patient Lost" February 22, 1966

Dr. Jeff Brenner overhears Orloff's offer to Noyes and Kildare and is later caught reading a car magazine by Gillespie. He later talks with Orloff about his practice.

Kildare talks with Barlow about her case and its effect on her dancing. Gillespie reviews her case and agrees with Noyes that Barlow should be dismissed.

181. "What Happened to All the Sunshine and Roses?" February 28, 1966

Mrs. Orloff tells Kildare that she is pregnant while asking if either he or Noyes will take over her husband's practice. Orloff is overjoyed when he finds out about the pregnancy. Meanwhile, Brenner goes to look over Orloff's clinic.

Gillespie and Kildare discuss Orloff's case and Kildare reads some books on neurology. Orloff offers Blair's interns a chance to buy his practice

182. "The Taste of Crow" March 7, 1966

Orloff and Kildare discuss a case similar to Barlow's and Kildare says that patient turned out to have myasthenia gravis. Barlow cleans up after a party and talks with her friend Jaime Angel about needing to dance.

Gillespie tells Brenner that he won't be getting a residency at Blair, and then watches Dr. Max Gunther run tests on Barlow. The tests reveal that she has myasthenia gravis. Barlow takes an overdose of pills after telling Noyes, who revealed the diagnosis to her, to leave her room.

183. "Out of a Concrete Tower" March 8, 1966

Orloff and Angel discuss Barlow's suicide attempt. Orloff then confronts Noyes, telling him he's a lousy doctor, after which he has another attack.

Gillespie and Kildare examine Orloff while his family watches. Mrs. Orloff and Noyes discuss the Barlow case after which Noyes goes to see Barlow at her school where Cavelli, the owner, wants her to be an instructor. Noyes then decides to buy Orloff's practice.

Writer: Archie L. Tegland.

Director: Alf Kjellin.

Also appearing in this arc were Jack Nicholson, Robert Cornthwaite, Michael Panareff, Helen Kleeb and Bruce Hyde. Hyde also worked with Shatner on *Star Trek*.

184. "The Art of Taking a Powder" March 14, 1966

Restaurant owner Bruno Rossi (Joe de Santis) refuses treatment and tries to leave Blair. While Kildare is trying to comfort Mrs. Rossi, their son Richard Ross, an actor (John Saxon) is coming home to see his father.

Lawton submits her resignation to Mrs. Fain while Ross plans to stay until his father's death. Gillespie tells Lawton that she is a valued employee and asks if she is leaving nursing. She tells Kildare that she is leaving because of an illness in her family.

185. "Read the Book, See the Movie" March 15, 1966

Kildare tells Ross that his father can't be moved. Ross then examines the car that his friend Stack Vernon (Lawrence Casey) drove from New York to California. Ross later takes his father from the hospital to see the new car.

Lawton tells Gillespie that she is leaving because she loves Kildare. Ross goes to his father's restaurant and asks his brother (Lawrence Montaigne) for a loan. Kildare tells Ross that his father is in and out of a coma and Rossi awakens one last time. Lawton tells Kildare that she is staying at Blair.

Writer: Jerry De Bono.

Director: Herschel Daugherty.

Also featured in this arc were Joan Marshall and Angela Clarke.

186. "A Sometimes Distant Spring" March 21, 1966

Claire Hanson passes out while fixing dinner for Kildare and Lawton. Gillespie and Kildare examine Hanson while Lawton stays with her daughter Margaret.

Kildare suggests Hanson get surgery for her heart condition. Lawton tells Kildare how the Hansons met while they were in college.

187. "Travel a Crooked Road" March 22, 1966

Hanson passes out while at her new job in a bookstore. Gillespie tells her she needs the surgery Kildare discussed with her. Claire decides to get the operation done before her husband, a soldier who escaped from a POW camp, returns home.

Gillespie tells Hanson that her speech centers were affected by the surgery. Lawton and Kildare discuss the case over lunch at Mac's. Kildare tells Claire what David Hanson went through and that they need each other's help.

188. "Mercy—or Murder?" March 28, 1966

Kildare and Dr. Vincent Brill (Mart Hulswit) are part of a TV panel discussion on abortion. After the show, Kildare and Brill go to the latter's apartment where Kildare takes a call for Brill.

Gillespie tells Kildare that both he and Brill should have been more discreet in their remarks. Meanwhile, Brill tries (with her landlady's help) to get into the apartment of Madeline Scott, a woman who called about getting an abortion even though Brill suggested that she put her baby up for adoption.

Lt. Dan Hargrave (Murray Hamilton) tells Blair's staff about finding a dead body in a "health studio" and says they're looking for Madeline Scott.

189. "Strange Sort of Accident" March 29, 1966

Kildare and Brill argue about Madeline Scott. Hargrave and his partner, Sgt. Hensley, question Brill with Hargrave asking him about $600 found in his apartment.

Brill bumps into an old friend, Rev. Jack Elder (Richard Beymer) after an argument with Kildare. Gillespie tells Brill that he's suspended from duty until his arraignment. Elder invites Brill to practice in the small town of Alder's Green when Brill says he's resigned from Blair. DA Prince tells Gillespie that Brill will be charged with felony murder.

190. "New Doctor In Town" April 4, 1966

Elder shows Brill around the town of Alder's Green while his wife sets up a date for Brill. Dr. Andrew Bennett (Sidney Blackmer), Brill's new boss, asks about his situation and introduces Fred Canford, the town's other doctor.

191. "Reckoning" April 5, 1966

Brill (on Elder's suggestion) takes Laurel Collins to church where Brill preaches a sermon about the true meaning of love. Kildare comes to see Laurel, who is actually Madeline Scott, the woman Brill tried to help while he was on staff at Blair.

Writer: Edward J. Lakso.

Director: John Brahm.

Also featured in this episode arc were George Kennedy, Edward Binns, Harry Townes, Shannon Farnon, Melanie Alexander, Audrey Totter, Diane Varsi, Kym Korath, Virginia Gregg and Ruth Hall. The music for the arc was composed by John Green.

§

Index

CPSIA information can be obtained at www.ICGtesting.com
Printed in the USA
BVOW06s2153170816

459375BV00013B/101/P